Never
to
Return

Never to Return

SANDY REID

BLACK & WHITE PUBLISHING

First published 2008
by Black & White Publishing Ltd
29 Ocean Drive, Edinburgh EH6 6JL

1 3 5 7 9 10 8 6 4 2   08 09 10 11 12

ISBN: 978 1 84502 223 5

A CIP catalogue record for this book is available from the British Library.

Typeset by RefineCatch Limited, Bungay, Suffolk
Printed and bound by Norhaven A/S, Denmark

For Chloe

The moon sailed high in the winter sky,
The treetops swayed in the breeze,
The travellers slept in their warm bow tents,
While outside all did freeze.
They were warm, they were happit,
All snugly wrapped and braw,
When the sounds of the night were shattered,
By the shrill of an auld black craw.
Richt abeen her heid he sat, twa claws on the hazel bough,
She lookit up, an pricked her lugs, as he said listen now,
A wednae tell a lie tae ye, ye ken a bring bad news,
They'll mak oot like they're friendly, but lassie that's a ruse.
Tak up yer tent, an hazels bent, an mak richt oot this wood,
An hold that road, an dae look back, that's if ye ken whit's good,
A canna hang aboot noo lass, tak heed tae whit a say,
Or the bairns ye hold sae close tae ye, you'll hold fer yin mair day!

Introduction

My mother, Mary Stewart, was born on 19th June 1923 in a woodcutter's shed at Dalguise, near Dunkeld. She was the eldest daughter of David (Dytes) Stewart and Martha (Peasie) Reid, Scottish tinkers who led a nomadic life in rural Perthshire. Having no permanent home, the Stewarts lived in tents and were often to be seen camped in woods or at the roadside, as they wandered the countryside in their constant search for work. They offered their labour on farms, sold their wares round doors, and readily turned their hand to anything that could supplement their meagre income. Dytes, the itinerant tinsmith, was welcomed at almost every cottage door, as was his wife Martha, carrying her basket of wares and herbal remedies. Tinker families were very close knit and sociable and the Stewarts would often travel in the company of other close relatives. There was a large extended family and Mary had many friends and relatives that she could call upon and visit.

The origins of tinkers have been lost in the mists of time. Skills that had been honed through the centuries and passed from father to son had enabled David Stewart to become a craftsman that could fashion anything from tin, wood, bone or horn. But, with each passing year, the skills of the tinker were becoming more and more obsolete in a rapidly changing world. The notion of a free spirit wandering the open road where the earth is his carpet and the stars are his roof is both romantic and fanciful. In reality the life of a tinker could be harsh, raw and sometimes very cruel. Music, songs, and the sharing of tales round roaring campfires did not put food in the mouths of hungry women and children – only work could do that.

Many tinkers were illiterate but my mother was fortunate enough to attend school where she was taught to read and write. In theory, this should have created more opportunities and paved the way for a better way of life for the younger generation of tinkers at that time. But, as she was to discover, even educated tinkers still lived on the fringes of mainstream society. A society that was fast becoming fearful of a way of life that was different and increasingly prejudiced to the tinker's plight. The authorities tried to encourage younger tinkers to forsake their ancient way of life. And, with little or no work to be had in the countryside, many migrated to towns and cities where they were encouraged to take up permanent residence in houses. But many others of the older generation were reluctant to do this despite the consequences and hardships this was to bring. A way of life was over but it would not disappear quietly.

This is our story.

'I'm weary Henry – can we not be moving?'

'I've put word to your brother Davie, he'll be round with the pony to shift us, Mary.'

'It's getting on – you know was he peeving [*drinking*]?'

'Aye, but he's sick with the peeve now and swore blind he would shift us.'

The older boys had raked the dump and returned with their spoils. Mary was usually interested in whatever her sons managed to salvage, but not today.

'We can make off with what we can carry, put down behind a dyke for the night, a wee fire and we'll be fine – I'm not for this wood anymore Henry.'

'There's no sense to that Mary, we'll be away first thing tomorrow once the boys are off the peeve.' He was weary with her nagging.

It was with trepidation and a heavy heart that Mary put the children to sleep that night. She cradled her youngest son in her arms as the older boys cracked to their father round the fire and she remembered her mother's words:

'Fife! That's the worst place in the world for taking bairns away. You're better to see the winter out here in Dunkeld lassie.'

Everyone retired for the night. The boys had their own wee tent and the girls got in with the younger bairns.

'Are you no sleeping Ma?' It was her daughter Mary.

'I'm seeing to the bairn.'

'Is he alright Ma?'

'Aye he's fine, just a wee bit restless, now get your head down.'

'Night Ma.'

'Goodnight lassie.'

Mary had grown up on stories. As a child she would sit with her brothers and sisters round roaring campfires listening to family and friends. They told tales of long-dead relatives and this kept their memory alive in the hearts and minds of the children. Some stories were about good and evil and their own history and culture was taught this way. Some were of a more sinister nature and bore a supernatural theme, but the ones that really sent a shiver down Mary's spine were the tales of the Burkers.

Burkers were feared by every single living traveller. It was said that they prowled lonely lanes and woods at night looking for people to seize and kill. The corpses fetched a decent price when sold on for medical research. Drunkards leaving city bars, tramps lying in farm outbuildings and tinkers camped in lonely woods were prime targets. The adults used these stories to strike the fear of God into their children and hoped they would never wander far from the safety of the camp. As a child Mary would hide her head under the blankets after hearing such tales.

Burkers no longer roamed freely but there were still people out there who tinkers had good reason to fear. These people had no interest in adults – their targets were tinker children and they were known as the Welfare. The younger the child, the less likely they were to run back to their family and if the

Welfare got you early enough the chances of seeing your family again were very slim.

'Fife! That's the worst place in the world for taking bairns away.' Her mother's words came back again.

Late in the night the sound Mary dreaded reached her ears. The crack of a frozen stick, snapped not by an animal, but by a human foot! They were here and they were after the children.

'There's people in the wood Henry – wake up!' She gave him a shake.

'What's bothering you now?' He rubbed his bleary eyes.

'There's people in the wood!'

'People – what people?'

'I can hear them.'

'It's likely poachers, Mary.'

'No – it might be the Welfare looking to see if we have bairns here.'

'Don't be daft, go back to sleep and stop worrying woman!'

More sticks snapped and this time Henry heard them too. 'Jings, you're right Mary – there is people about!' He jumped to his feet as Mary wakened the children.

They were on the tents quickly and there was no time to do anything. Henry lifted the front flap and looked out. He had to shield his eyes from the bright torchlight that shone in his face. 'Who are you? What do you want?' he shouted.

'It's the police!' a voice boomed. 'We have the Welfare with us. We don't mean any harm and just want to make sure the children are ok.'

'Aye they're fine, and they were all sleeping before you lot came crashing in about!'

Henry noticed that the older boys had come from their tent.

'Stay back,' another policeman shouted to them, 'or we'll lift you.'

The boys watched anxiously.

A Welfare woman came forward. 'I just want to see that the children are ok.'

'I've already told you they're fine.'

'Yes, but I need to make sure Mr Reid.'

'Stand aside while I take a look in the tent,' the policeman insisted.

Henry stood back and he shone his torch inside. Mary sat with her youngest daughter on her knee. 'Who's that you have there?' he asked.

'Maggie – she's my youngest lassie . . .'

They were all ordered out the tent and stood in the freezing cold. The policeman flashed his torch around then came out. 'That's them all,' he said.

The head Welfare woman spoke next.

'Mrs Reid, we already have four of your children – why on earth do you keep having more? You're not in a position to look after them – they need to be in a warm bed, in a warm house, not some freezing tent in a wood!'

'They're fine and warm in the tent.'

'But look at them – they're shivering with cold!'

'That's because you have them standing in the freezing frost.'

The woman got impatient. 'What's the little girl's name?'

'Maggie.'

'What age is she?'

'Four.'

'She'll be ready to start the school next year – have you thought about that?'

'Aye.'

The woman sighed. 'A child needs proper education Mrs Reid and she's unlikely to get that if she's left with you. She'll need to come with us.'

'No . . . you can't take her away!' She held Maggie tight to her chest.

'Officer!'

The policeman came forward and tried to take Maggie.

'You're not taking her!' Mary shouted.

'If you don't hand her over I'll arrest you for breaching the peace.'

'We're better to do what they say Mary or they'll lift us both and take them all in.' Henry took his daughter and handed her to the Welfare woman.

'You can come to the County Buildings and we'll let you know how she is. Now you'd better get the rest of them back in the tent and out the cold.'

Just then the worst thing imaginable happened.

'What was that?' the Welfare woman asked.

'It's our cat,' Mary was quick to answer.

'A cat? It sounded more like a baby crying to me Mrs Reid. Have another look in the tent, Officer!'

The policeman went back in the tent and shone his torch and when he came out he had a little baby boy in his arms. 'He was under a pile of blankets right at the back – I must have missed him!'

Mary lunged forward and tried to take her son but quickly found her arms pinned to her sides by another policeman. 'Don't take him – he's only a baby,' she pleaded.

The Welfare woman took the boy.

'Don't take my baby – don't take him from me . . .'

'I have to take him Mrs Reid.' She started to walk away with the child in her arms.

'Are you a mammy – do you have children of your own?'

The woman stopped and looked over her shoulder. 'If I had children they would certainly not be living in a tent in a freezing wood Mrs Reid!'

The policeman loosened his grip as Mary fell to her knees. 'My baby . . . please give me back my baby . . .'

Her husband and sons came to her now.

'Make them give him back Henry . . . Don't let them take my wee boy . . .'

David, her eldest son, tried to comfort her but she rejected his advance and kept her eyes firmly fixed on the Welfare woman. She pointed her finger and hissed . . .

'Woe to he that would share your bed,
And implant the seed of life,
You'll never call a child your own,
For there goes no man's wife!'

The ashen-faced policeman withdrew and quickly followed the others out of the wood.

Henry finally spoke. 'We'll get round to the County Buildings first thing in the morning and check on the bairns Mary.'

'We'll never see them again Henry.'

And she was right. I never saw my mother again.

Balcarres

A good place to start would be with my very first memory and that takes me back to when I was about four years old. It was the scream my seven-year-old sister gave out that was to stick with me all these years. She'd just been whacked full force on her hand with a cane and the man who did it was my foster father. I can't remember what it was for but I got it first, a couple of wee baby taps that wouldn't hurt a flea and that's what put Maggie off her guard as she must have expected the same. By the time she'd finished doing the Highland fling he'd gone from the room.

My foster father was about thirty-five and had a face like a ferret. We'd ended up with a foster family because the Welfare wanted to get us out of the children's home and placed with a foster family so that we could have as normal an upbringing as possible, but I don't think they really knew what went on or how hard it could be sometimes for children that were boarded out. As Maggie was finding out. But, for the Welfare, the main thing was making sure that we were away from our parents and away from the tinker's life which they thought was so bad.

'Bastard!' Maggie swore. 'C'mon, we'll go outside.'

We left the room and made our way quietly along the hall and out the front door where the other bairns were waiting for

9

us. Sheena, Lizzie, Wullie, and Rab were our foster parents' natural children. The oldest was Wullie at eleven years of age, with Sheena aged ten, Lizzie aged eight and the youngest was Rab at seven years of age. Even for them there was not a lot of love to be had in that cold, drab place.

'Did you get the cane?' Rab asked, wiping green snot from his nose with his sleeve. He was the same age as Maggie and had inherited his father's ferret features.

'Just one,' Maggie said, blowing into her hands.

'That's bugger all, I got near a hundred once, no just on my hands but the backs o my legs too.'

'Shut your pus Rab!' his sister Sheena hissed. She was a sullen girl with unkempt mousy brown hair which her father cut himself. He cut everyone's hair including his own. Both my foster parents worked and as well as their own wages they had the money that the Welfare paid them for our keep, but that man would do anything to save a few quid.

We wandered off to the pond but before long, Jim, a tractor man from one of the farms, stopped beside us with a warning.

'Don't be walking out on that ice,' he shouted. 'It'll no take yer weight.'

'Aye, we'll bide off it,' Sheena roared back. He drove off and his collie dog was quick to follow the tractor after a kick in the ribs from Rab.

We all leaned on the wooden fence that surrounded the pond. Wullie pulled a piece and jam from his pocket.

'Where did you get that?' Rab asked.

'I sneaked it when they were getting a hiding.'

'Give us half.'

'No!'

'Go on, give us half o' it,' Rab pleaded, but was ignored.

We were always starving. Every single day we got the same thing to eat – white tripe – and it was horrible stuff. My foster mother would boil the tripe in a big pot and that was our staple diet – boiled white tripe! There was no favouritism for their own children but I really hated having to eat tripe all the time. But it was a clear choice, even at the age of four – you either ate what was in your bowl, no matter how horrible it was, or you went hungry. Sometimes my foster father didn't care if I ate the stuff or not. Other times, for some inexplicable reason, he would fly into a rage and force me to eat. His method was to to pinch my nose with two fingers, then hold my head back and literally ram the tripe down my gullet as I gagged.

To help give us a bit more variety in our diet, my sister would always try to pinch someone's play piece at school if she got the chance and if she managed to do that then she'd bring it home to share with me. That was a real treat. At other times she would rake the bins in the school playground and salvage whatever the other bairns had thrown away and bring it back to share with me. We were so hungry that we'd just about eat anything, no matter what it was or where it had been.

One time she was caught with her hands in someone's schoolbag and was reported to the headmaster. It was the afternoon when they got her and the headmaster said he would deal with her the following day. The next morning after assembly she was called up onto the stage and belted in front of the whole school. Just because she'd been hungry.

I had no memory of life with our parents, of course, having been taken by the Welfare when I was just a baby but Maggie, being a bit older, could remember what it was like. She knew that although we may not have had much, we never went hungry. We came from a close-knit family who loved us and Maggie certainly loved me, and was determined to try to lessen her little brother's suffering by any means possible, and at any cost.

Wullie's piece and jam looked very tempting to all of us and suddenly Rab made a snatch for it. But all he managed to do was knock it clean out of Wullie's hand and right out onto the ice.

'You wee bugger.' Wullie swung a punch but missed and Rab ran behind Sheena. Wullie was furious but there was nothing he could do and so the piece was left where it landed on the ice. But the thought of that piece was really making my mouth water.

The pond was one of our favourite places and we used to swim there during the summer months. It wasn't deep. I was only a wee lad and it just came up to my waist, but at this time of the year the water would be freezing and you could catch your death of cold. But despite that, I had my eye on that piece!

All the children in the house had chores to do and my job every night was to go out and fill a big box with sticks for the fire. You had to wait until you were sent and that was always after dark. 'Away and get sticks and watch out for the ghosts,' he would say. Maybe he was trying to frighten me.

This night I was desperate to get out with the stick box and as soon as he told me to go and fetch them I headed out to the wood. It was a beautiful clear, freezing cold night and the sky was like crystal with millions of stars and a near full moon. The darkness held no fear for me thanks to my traveller back-ground – there wasn't a traveller boy living that had any fear of the dark – and even woods at night never bothered me. Maggie was always telling me who I was and where I came from, that we were travellers with parents who loved us and friends everywhere. Even at this young age, I had a strong sense of the traveller heritage and of who I was. And there was no way a wee bit of darkness was ever going to scare me, even if my foster father thought it would.

Collecting the sticks was the best job he could have given me and I always looked forward to getting out of the house. At first I would tear my hands to bits trying to rip branches from the trees in the pitch dark. But Maggie and the other kids were good at helping by leaving a few big piles of sticks deep in the wood so that I just had to go and collect them. This was a right cold night and I had only one thing in mind – to get to the pond as quick as I could. The frost crunched under my feet as I made my way up there and soon I was through the fence and prodding the ice with my foot to see if it would hold me. It did.

I could see the piece in the moonlight and it was only a few tantalising steps away. I very gently made my way across to it and bent to pick it up but it was stuck fast with the frost. I gave it a kick and there was a mighty crack, the ice split and I went clean through and was up to my waist in freezing water! My breath left me with the shock but I was out of that water in a flash, dripping and shivering and near blue with the cold. I shivered all the way back to the cottage having filled the box with sticks but I knew with every step that there would be some punishment coming my way.

He had no pity that night. He stood me in front of the open fire until the steam was coming off my trousers and the next day my legs were covered in blisters with the heat of the fire. It was shortly after that that I took the chilblains and that's the sorest thing in the world for a bairn. God knows how long I had them but there was always some kind of infection on my feet right through that winter. It was a miserable winter which seemed to last forever but they wouldn't take me to the doctor. The doctor had already written a letter to the Welfare saying he would not treat me or my sister any more. 'Too many accidents,' he had said and recommended to the Welfare that we be shifted, but they just left us where we were.

When we were first taken away we were put to a home called St David's in St Andrews, Fife. After that we were shifted further along the coast to a children's home called St

Margaret's in Elie. The Welfare then made a lonely children's appeal in the Sunday Pictorial asking if there was a family that could give us a good home and a couple from Huntingdon in England replied but they couldn't take us both. Thankfully, the Welfare said that we were to stay together and they eventually found us a foster family who would take both Maggie and me. It wasn't great, but at least we were together.

We lived in a cottage called the Laundry House on the Balcarres estate and were about a mile from the village of Colinsburgh, near Elie. My foster parents were both employed, him as a handyman and her as a cleaner and the house went with the job. He was an Englishman and he told us that the half of England was after him and that's why he came to Scotland where they couldn't get him. I thought he liked some odd things, like classical music and reading lots of books. I'd never heard classical music before then and it seemed an odd thing to like. He was also fond of a good drink and he got that at the Commercial Inn down in Colinsburgh. He'd also argue a lot and get into fights, which is what happened one night outside the Balcarres Arms in the main street of Colinsburgh.

Late one night, we were sent down to the village to see that he came home safe. He'd been away drinking for some time. When we got there, we opened the door of the Commercial Inn and the woman who ran the place told us to get out. 'He's no here and he'll no be back till I get the money he owes me – you'll get him across the road.'

The Balcarres Arms was on the other side of the road and up a wee bit from the Commercial so off we went. But he wouldn't come out and we were left standing at the door with two or three other bairns from the village. Then an argument started between Rab and this other boy and Rab ended up on his arse when the lad punched him. That was like a red rag to a bull for Sheena and she flew on the boy and was kicking his brains out when a man came out the pub. It turned out that he was a relative of the boy and he grabbed Sheena by the neck and gave her a slap. Rab shot into the pub and got his father who flew out the pub door and got stuck in. By the time he'd finished with him, the blood was pouring like a river from the man's face.

But that still wasn't the end of it. Soon more men were pouring out of the pub and a huge brawl was underway. They were rolling about on the road and the coppers were falling out of their pockets and we went round picking them up. We had tanners, threepenny bits, pennies and halfpennys, but I picked up the best one – a half crown! Eventually, the men just exhausted themselves, wiped off the blood and staggered off home. Another eventful night in Colinsburgh!

The next day all the bairns were at school and the foster people were away to work so I wandered down to the village with my new-found wealth and went into the shop. I got a big bag of sweets with all kinds of stuff in it like penny chews, bars of chocolate and a pie packed with meat – and it was good meat, not like the tripe we got at home. I remember eating the whole lot in one go and it was the best I'd ever eaten. Thinking back, there weren't so many good days in that place but that was one I'll never forget.

There were some good things about the estate we lived on, like old Tam Anderson. He lived in a bothy not far from our house and he never took out his ashes. He had been fighting in the war and a bomb had blown half his brains out and his skull had all been stitched up. We would do wee jobs for him and for that you would get a big bowl of soup. I've no idea what he made his soup from but it was always much tastier than anything my foster mother managed to make.

Anytime you went near his place he'd say, 'Halt – who goes there?' He had a long grey beard that was nearly down to the belt round his waist and he never changed his breeks which were black and caked with dirt.

Tam's dog was called Jet and it was the laziest dog in the world. It hardly ever moved from the fire. Any time we were at Tam's bothy, we'd take out the ashes, bring in some sticks for the fire and clean up the bothy before we sat down to eat our soup.

And every time we were there he'd shout at the dog, 'Will you move from the fire till we get a heat.' But it paid him no heed. Then one day he went over and gave Jet a kick but it never flinched. So he grabbed it by the neck and it just hung limp. 'The bugger's dead!' he shouted, and he told us it must have eaten the rat poison that he'd put down. He asked us to make a big fire at the back of the bothy and that's where he burnt Jet. It was a sad moment for old Tam, even though he'd managed to kill his own dog with rat poison. A few days later I was back up there when nobody was about and the bones of the poor old dog were still lying there in the cold ashes.

One way to stop a cat spitting at you is to split it with an axe and that's exactly what Rab did to one of the farm tabbies. We were chopping kindling and it came from behind some tattie sacks and was hissing and spitting like it was mad, so Rab near cut the thing in two and threw it in the woods. It was a cruel thing to do and I didn't think it was funny.

By the time we finished in the woodshed it was getting dark and we saw a car coming up the dirt track. We held back and watched a woman get out wearing a tweed suit and carrying a briefcase. She went up to the door and gave three knocks. Sheena let her in and we followed at the back of her.

My foster parents had asked for money to buy extra blankets for the winter and when that came through they went off to Edinburgh. That was when the woman arrived and they were still away when she turned up at the door. The woman explained that she was from the Welfare and had come out to see us.

'Are you the oldest?' she asked Sheena.

'No, Wullie is, but I'm left in charge for he's no capable.'

'I see,' she said, writing a note in a wee book. She was a dull kind of woman and looked like some of the women you would see coming out the church on a Sunday. She asked Maggie if she liked the school and she said that she did. Then she looked at me and asked if I had been behaving, but I never let on to her and she never bothered to ask me anything else.

'When will your parents be back Sheena?'

'In the morning.'

'Tomorrow?' She had a look of concern on her face.

'Aye, they're away through to Edinburgh to get blankets.'

'Why Edinburgh? Can't they get blankets in Leven or Kirkcaldy – that's much closer?'

'Aye, but if you want good thick ones you have to go to Edinburgh.'

The woman asked Sheena to show her round the cottage and when she came back we had lost interest in her and were throwing sticks on the fire. Maggie was scratching away at her head and the woman said, 'Does the school nurse check your head Maggie?'

'Aye, but she tears lumps out my skull so I don't like it.'

'But you need to have it checked regularly.'

'Aye.'

I had my boots off and I could see the woman looking at my chilblained feet.

'Your feet look very sore Sandy – have you got ointment for them?' she asked.

I looked at Sheena, who was standing behind the Welfare woman with a finger pressed to her lips. So I never answered and the woman just wrote more stuff in her book. Then she got fed up with us and went away.

The next day my foster father said nobody was to ever get in the house when he was away, not even the Welfare, and

Sheena got a few slaps round the ear for letting the social worker in.

One of my jobs was to feed the hens and make sure that they had fresh water every day. Well, this day there were feathers and bits of hen lying all over the place and I knew that a fox had got to them. I looked to see if there were any eggs in the hen hut and I got about the same amount as usual. There was still a good few hens going about the place so I decided not to say anything about it to my foster father.

I was trying to fix the fence as best I could when a woman came walking up the path. She was from the big house and spoke with a toffee nose, but she was a good enough woman and would always stop and speak to me. This woman took lots of walks and this day she had on a big long coat and a pair of Wellington boots. She wore a fox fur round her neck like a scarf. I told her about the fox getting to the hens and she said she would tell one of the men to shoot it if he saw it going about and I said that would make another good scarf for her. Then she took this bent yellow thing from her pocket and gave it to me.

'What's that?' I asked, and she said it was a banana. I had no clue what to do with it so she took it back and peeled the skin off and took a bite herself before handing it back to me. And that was the first banana I'd ever seen or tasted in my life. Mind you, I wolfed it down so quickly that I hardly tasted it anyway.

When I finished with the fence I heard the noise of a big petrol saw. I went through the woods and when I got to the woodcutter he was so busy working that he didn't notice me approaching. I could see his piece bag lying nearby on a tree stump, so I went into his bag and pinched the sandwiches. This was the first thing I can remember intentionally stealing in my life, but I was so hungry that I had no scruples about taking the woodcutter's sandwiches. Looking back, I'm not sure I was really stealing at all – it was survival.

From there I made my way to Tam's bothy and he put on a drop tea and I shared the sandwiches with him. He would certainly have known that my foster family had not given me any kind of packed lunch but he never bothered to ask me where I got the sandwiches and just helped me to gobble them up. And they were really good.

Tam was always good for telling stories and you heard plenty about the war he'd fought in. He knew all about guns and would show me how to work one using a big stick. It was the machine gun corps he was in and lots of his mates were killed and when he came back from the fighting there were bits of him missing and he only had six fingers left from the ten he started with. I liked spending time with him and hearing about all the things that had happened to him. Nothing much seemed to happen to me so it was exciting to listen to his stories and dream about what I might get up to in the future. As usual, after a while, when the sandwiches were finished and the stories told, he fell asleep and I went off to find something else to do.

Now as you get older you might think that time can go quick, but it can also go very slow and for my mother this particular day had dragged. She had arrived at the County Buildings in Cupar at nine o'clock in the morning and the clock on the wall told her that it was now half past two in the afternoon. Social workers came and went. Other visitors arrived, were seen, and left but no one paid any attention to the tinker woman waiting patiently on a wooden chair. She knew that to complain would not be in her interest. If she complained or made any kind of fuss they would simply have her removed from the building and she would not be given any information about her children. She also knew that if she waited long enough then someone would eventually have to come and speak to her. Simply to hear from someone in authority that her children were doing well and were happy would have been well worth the wait for Mary Reid. But she was to be denied even this small comfort when my father staggered into the building.

'For fuck's sake Henry!' She took him by the arm and got him quickly past the folk and out the building. 'I told you not to come here!'

'Did . . . did you see the bairns Mary . . . ?' he slurred.

'No, I never saw them, and I'm not likely to see them with the carry-on you keep – you're shaming me man!'

They got to the park and sat down. There were other tinkers in the park and they were all drinking.

'Away and beg some coppers for another bottle of wine Mary.'

She ignored her husband's request and set her eyes on an old hedge-hopper who was coming in about. It was Danny O'Reilly, an old tramp, who was filthy and reeked to high heaven.

'Have you any coppers Danny?' Henry asked him, but the man had nothing.

Choking for more drink, my father quickly became aggressive and ended up giving my mother a punch in the face.

She left the park with no option but to try and get some money and begged a man in the main street. It turned out that he was an American.

'What happened to your eye?' he asked.

'I fell.'

'You should see a doctor, it might need a stitch.'

'I'm alright.'

'Take this,' He pulled a hanky from his pocket. Mary looked at the three letters on it and they read WWP.

'William W Perkins the third. That's me.'

'That's a right fancy name you have.'

'What's your name?' he asked.

'Mary.'

'Pleased to meet you Mary,' He shook her hand, and she offered the hanky back, but he said to keep it. The man didn't seem to care that Mary was a tink and he took her into a cafe. He bought tea and biscuits and cracked with her for a while.

'I need to be out begging the price of a drink,' Mary said.

'I like a drink myself,' he said, and took her across the road to a pub. Two malt whiskies were ordered and Mary put the drink down her neck so he would not be offended. He put up more whisky and more yet, and Mary started a song.

> I've no got muckle,
> Can you give me a puckle,
> For a puckle can be muckle,
> When you're poor . . .

That's the way the song went and the American loved it and asked her to sing more. They got drunk and the man bought two whole bottles of whisky to take away, for he never bothered about money. Mary took him to the park where they had a good fire going and everyone was pleased to meet my mother's new friend.

He told them about America and they all listened. The tinkers had heaps of songs and stories of their own and put on a wee ceilidh for the man and he was right pleased with it all. After about two hours the police came and tried to put a stop to it, but all they got was cheek. So everyone was ordered out the park and when they stayed put they all got lifted.

The next day they were put before the Sheriff and he fined them all three pounds. The American paid all the fines, then promptly disappeared and that was the last they saw of him.

* * *

A place called the Serpentine lies between Upper and Lower Largo and that's where my mother and father went next. My Uncle Sandy had a camp there and in front of the camp you had the railway line and the sea further yet. Sandy and his wife Peggy were pleased to see them and they had news.

'Two of the bairns – Maggie and Sandy – are boarded out. The Balcarres Estate is where you'll get them. They bide in a cottage up there and Maggie goes to the wee school in Colinsburgh.'

'Who told you that Sandy?' Mary asked.

'A fisherman from Pittenweem – he has a brother works the estate and he saw the bairns were tinks and gave their names to me.'

'I wouldn't go up to the cottage Mary – they'll put the police onto you,' Peggy said.

'Aye, she's right,' Sandy went on. 'You could maybe just catch Maggie at the school.'

At this point, Mary had spent two years trying to find her bairns. She was never done visiting the County Buildings in Cupar. She had posted many letters to the Welfare, but seldom, if ever, was she to be given any useful information about them. Now, thanks to her brother Sandy, she knew where two of her children were.

That evening, as she walked along the beach with Peggy, they came across another tinker woman. You would take this woman for about a hundred and ten, but she was only fifty-five years of age and her name was Isabella. She told them that her man had landed in jail and that she was weary and that she could not stop walking. They offered to take her back to the camp for the night, but the woman just kept going.

The next morning it rained. Colinsburgh was about three miles away and they hung about in the main street when they got there.

'There's nothing happens here,' Henry said at length.

'Aye, but we need to wait until the school comes out for dinner.'

'What time will that be, Mary?' He was bored.

'I'll ask this woman coming along.' But the woman crossed the street and ignored them. This didn't bother my mother or Peggy. They were both used to being shunned by people.

The man from the Balcarres Arms came out and Henry and Sandy went over to him. They chatted for several minutes then went inside with him.

'They'll be working the man for the price of a drink,' Mary said.

A fat woman came along and she could hardly get a breath. 'This walk to the shop just about kills me,' she gasped.

'What time does the school take their dinner?' Mary asked.

'One o'clock.'

'That's a while yet.'

'Are you waiting for someone?'

'Aye.'

The woman got the shop and stopped again. 'Do you tell fortunes?'

'Aye,' said Mary, and they were invited to her house.

After the fortune telling, the women went back to wait near the school. Suddenly there was a commotion further up the street.

'Fuck off – or I'll set the dogs on you!' It was the man from the pub.

Henry and Sandy crossed the street.

'What's he raging about Henry?' Mary asked.

'He thinks we pinched money from the place.'

'Did you?'

'No, he's moich [*mad*].'

They got to the school and the bairns were all in the play-ground.

'That's her over there, the one with the blue coat – Maggie!'
Mary shouted.

Maggie came over to the black railings and knew her
mother right away. 'Is that you Ma?'

'Aye it's me.'

'Have you come to take me back Ma?' Maggie was so
pleased to see her mother and could hardly contain her joy.
But just then a police car screeched to a halt and the constable had the man from the pub with him.

'Come here you lot – and turn out your pockets!'

Other school bairns had joined Maggie at the railings and
were watching the spectacle now.

'What's up?' Henry asked.

'Just turn out your pockets!'

'What for?'

'Do you want lifted?'

'No.'

'Then let's see what you have!'

They all emptied their pockets and he took the two shillings
that Mary had been given for the fortune telling.

'That's my own money!' she protested.

'Shut up!'

'You can ask the woman that gave me it.'

'I said shut up!' He sorted through the rest of their stuff.

'What's he doing Ma?' My sister was anxious.

The policeman looked at Maggie. 'Away and play lassie, this
is none of your business!'

'I'll speak to you in a minute once he's finished with us,'
Mary said to Maggie.

'Right,' said the constable when he'd looked through everything, 'get your arses out this village and don't let me see your
faces round here again.'

The men wandered slowly away but Mary tried to speak to
her daughter again.

'I told you to shift!' the policeman said, rapidly losing patience.

'Can I just have a wee word with my lassie please?'

'Shift! Now! Or I'll lift you!'

There was nothing else for it but to move on. It was a bitter blow to just get a few words before having to leave and Mary was very upset. They walked down to Elie where they sat in silence in the bus shelter across from the church.

'There's a good wee grocer shop here,' Henry finally said, taking off his boot. Mary watched as he gave it a shake and three folded ten-shilling notes fell out.

'You did take money from that man!' She was angry.

'Aye.'

'And I never got seeing the bairn for that.'

'You'll see her another time.'

'Bastard!'

When the men came out the grocer's, they downed the first bottle of wine in the street. Then they all went down to the beach and the women took a drink as well. Later the two women begged the street and they got more wine. When they returned, a fire was blazing and they roared and squabbled until they got tired and fell asleep on the sand.

Maggie was both happy and sad when I saw her again later. It was the first time she had seen her mother for years and all she really wanted was to hug her and be with her, even for a few minutes. But Henry had put paid to that. It was a bitter blow for us both but at least it gave us hope that maybe, one day, they'd come for us.

Although I was only four years old, I would often be left to fend for myself during the day. My sister and the other children would set off for the school in Colinsburgh, and both my foster parents had their work to go to. When everyone left in the morning, the cottage door was locked and I would be left sitting alone on the cold stone doorstep. This particular morning it rained hard, so I sheltered in the woodshed next to the cottage. In the afternoon, when the rain stopped, I decided to leave the woodshed and make my way down to the big house. When I got there, I went round the side to the kitchen and saw the cook who gave me a cup of milk and a ginger biscuit. Then I went to the gardens and found Roger. He was a grown man, but had the brains of a bairn and even I had more sense than him. Roger was always pleased to see me. He would make out he was a soldier at the time of the war but that was just lies. And he always had a spade in his hand but I never saw him digging.

'I'll show you something,' he says, and pulls a photograph from his pocket. 'That's me in my soldier's uniform.'

'That's not you, that's your dad,' I said.

'Aye, you're right, but folk say I look just like him.'

I looked at the picture then looked back at him. 'You could near take you for him.'

'That's right.'

'You're as like as two peas.'

'He's dead now.'

'Aye.'

'Killed by the Germans.'

'Aye.'

'And I miss him.'

'Aye.'

He started crying so I left him to it and went off to the walled garden. This was one of my favourite places and I sat down on a wooden seat and looked at the big house. I thought there must be about a million rooms in it. We were all crammed into one small cottage where we seemed to trip over each other due to lack of space. Maggie would often tell me about the tents that we lived in before the Welfare took us away, and I imagined that the tents would be even smaller than the cottage that we lived in now. I wished that my family did not live in tents. If they had a big house like this, then we would not have been taken away and we would still be together. That way my sister would not feel so bad, and if Maggie was happy then I knew that I would be happy too. But sitting and playing in this walled garden wasn't so bad.

It wasn't long before my foster father got word from the headmaster about my parents being at the school. He was raging. He always said, 'If a job's worth doing you have to do it right,' and, true to his word, he gave Maggie a right good hiding. She got the blame for them being at the school and he got onto the Welfare who said they would speak to the police about it.

I knew that if my parents hadn't gone to the school then my foster father would not have needed to give Maggie a hiding, and I hoped that they would never visit the school again, for Maggie's sake. As an adult, I would discover that my mother had taken matters even further and had written directly to my foster parents. On my social services file it states that 'Mrs Reid has written to foster parents – a long sad letter asking for photo etc. He is to reply to her – politely, but telling her he cannot conduct correspondence etc.'

It was near Christmas. I had chapped lips and it was snowing. I sat in the hut with the hens and when the snow stopped I came out. I liked snow but I didn't like it when it blew a blizzard. The woman from the big house was going about and she spoke to me.

'It will soon be Christmas,' she says.

'Aye.'

'You must be excited?'

'Aye.'

'Do you know anything about baby Jesus?'

I never answered.

'He was born on Christmas Day and that's why we celebrate.'

I didn't listen to her and started to walk away.

'Hold on,' she says, and pulls a pair of bright red mittens from her pocket. She puts them on my hands and tells me she knitted them herself and that they'll keep my fingers warm. They were queer things and you only had a thumb and no bits to move your fingers. That wasn't much use so, when she left, I threw them away.

I get back to the cottage and the rest of them are home in an hour. My foster father has cut a Christmas tree and they're putting stuff they made at school on it. I kindled the fire and went to get logs and they're still at this tree when I come back. I have a good blaze going and take the boots off my feet. They start to argue about where things should go on the tree and my foster father explodes and kicks the tree over and that's the end of it for now.

After he's eaten, my foster father's ready for the pub and he tells Rab and me to walk with him. We get to the village and he goes straight into the Balcarres Arms and we start to walk back to the cottage. There are boys playing at the end of the street and Rab challenges them. There are three of them and two of us and I get a punch that makes me dizzy and my nose starts to bleed. We have to run and when we get to the woods they don't follow and we're fine.

After the pub he's back with two men that I've never seen before. One gives two brown trout to my foster mother and the other one plays a fiddle. That man knew some good tunes and kept at it long after I was sent to bed. That was a good night and my foster father never bothered anybody.

It was a month after Christmas that the complaints started to come from the Royal Scottish Society for the Prevention of Cruelty to Children and that got my foster father absolutely raging. The Welfare came to see him and when he asked who complained they said that the complaints were anonymous. He said they were malicious and must have been made by people that didn't like him. He said he could get a good word from the police and also from his employer. That seemed to be fine with the Welfare and that was the end of it.

When they were all away I just mucked about and pleased myself. One morning I decided to go and see Tam in his bothy. This day he had some kind of fever and was in his box bed. He told me to get sticks and kindle a fire. Then he wanted some tea and I put the black kettle on the fire. When I turned round he was growling like a dog and his hands and feet were thrashing about in the bed. I paid him no heed and put the tea leaves in the pot and when he'd calmed down I took the tea to him and he smelt of pish. He wasn't his usual self so I left him to get on with it.

I went up the hill where there was an old ruin and you could see the sea from there. I came down a path and found Roger in a heap after falling from his bike. He still had on the jumper that he got for Christmas and it had snowmen on the front. He told me he'd started smoking and lit a woodbine. After a few puffs he was spluttering like old Tam and he threw the fag away. He never got back on the bike and we walked to the big house.

When we got to the kitchen, the cook put scones in front of us. Roger told her he'd come off his bike and she said he had to be more careful and not to go so fast. She told me to have another scone and said that I was far too thin. She was a big enough woman and you could tell she liked her own cooking and she was cheery and good hearted. Roger never needed to be told and just helped himself to anything he wanted.

'Away and check the mouse traps,' she said to Roger.

I went with him and we got two mice in the kitchen before

we went to check the hall. I left him to the traps and looked at the pictures that hung on the walls. Some of them were huge and needed a big house like this. Roger went different places and I was busy looking when the Earl came along. He asked me what I was doing and I said I was looking for mice and he said you won't find them on the walls. I was back with the cook when Roger came. He sat down and lit a woodbine and that got him kicked out the kitchen.

Sometimes if we kept a carry-on in the cottage we would be stripped to our underwear and made to stand outside in the freezing cold. Maggie would have to face the wall at one end of the cottage and I would have to face the wall at the other end. If it was really cold then you would be frozen like ice by the time he came for you. When your time was up at that you got a few whacks to your legs with a cane and that was sore.

Other times, you could land in the coal bunker, which was padlocked to keep you in. But sometimes my foster father would get really angry with me and then he would take me to the cave. The cave was an old ice house that was no longer in use and you'd to go a good bit through the wood to get to this cold damp place, and you got a real good hiding on the way. He would lower me by the arms down into this sunken hollow for I was far too little to get in by myself. If I looked up I could see the tops of the trees and the stars if they were out. I was never left for long in that cold rat-infested place, and if my foster father fell asleep at the fire then my foster mother would come for me and take me back to the warmth of the cottage. I hated all these punishments but the ice house was the worst.

One day I got word that old Tam had died and I was told by my foster father to stay away from his bothy. About a week later I decided to go and take a look at the place and found the door unlocked and everything just as Tam had left it. The place was cold so I took out the ashes and fetched kindling to light a fire. I got busy about the place and when there was nothing else to do I sat down to think about the old man and started to cry.

Mary sat at the fire and, looking about, had good reason to feel proud. My father had been sent to prison for nine months for various charges of dishonesty and assault. And in his absence she had managed to get herself a house. She had been off the drink for a while now and was hopeful the children would be returned to her soon. She kept good company and was attending services at the Gospel Mission in Dundee. Her son Davie was living with her so she was not alone. She had asked the Evangelical Gypsy Mission to write a letter in support of her application to have the children returned and they said this was something they could consider if she was baptized.

She had managed to get hold of some good secondhand furniture and had even found an old piano, which she quickly learned to play by ear. She liked the songs they sang at the mission house and Davie and her would often sing late into the night. She was eating well and paying regular instalments on the house and things were certainly looking up.

Money was still very tight though, so when the summer came they decided to go for the berry picking. They locked up the house in Dundee and set off for Blairgowrie. When they got to Blair there were people from everywhere going about and the place was teeming. Mary needed to get some groceries and left Davie cracking to some folk in the Wellmeadow. When she returned, Davie was with her cousin old Colin Stewart. Colin told them he was camped alongside old Dytes and Martha (my grandparents) and he walked with them back to the camp.

Martha and Dytes were pleased to see their daughter and quickly got all the news, especially about my dad.

'He's lying in Perth jail,' Mary said.

'Best place for that man,' her mother replied.

'Nine months he's doing. I have my own house in Dundee now and Davie's with me.'

'If you stick at it you might manage to get the bairns back Mary.'

'Aye, that's what I'm hoping for.'

'But you'll need to keep that man at arm's length.'

'I'll no be taking him back – that's me finished with him!'

As the evening wore on, more and more people gathered. Fires were lit, the bairns quietened and that's when the stories started. Old Colin had a good one.

'I was camped out by Brechin a month back and put the tent into a good bit with plenty grass and a bit bracken. I was just fine there, plenty wood for the fire, a wee burn for water, and nobody to bother you. After a few days one of the boys from the farm comes and says the farmer wants me to shift. Well, I never bothered my arse and just stayed where I was but the next morning when I looked out the camp I was face to face with a big bull! The eyes were all bloodshot and the slavers were hanging from its mouth and it looked a right mean bugger. The farmer had put him there to make me shift you see.

'Well I needed the shop in Brechin but as soon as you put a foot out the camp it would start stamping at the ground and wouldn't let you past. The only thing to do was to make a bolt for the fence, and that's what I did. I managed to dodge the beast and was running flat out for the fence with this mad bugger right on my heels. Well I gets over the fence and lands awkward on my ankle, and with nothing better to do the beast starts to wreck my camp!

'My ankle's sprained a bit and I'm lying in the long grass when two of the farm boys come to see what the carry-on is. They see the bull going berserk with the camp and me lying on the ground rubbing my ankle. "That bugger got me!" I shouts. "Put me right up in the air." They get the farmer and I tell him the bull got me. "Stay there till I come back," he says.

'He's away for about five minutes and when he gets back he hands me a fiver and a bottle of whisky! "Don't be mentioning this to anyone," he says, and he tells the men to fix the camp for me. He never wanted a complaint about the bull you see, and he took the beast away and said I could sit for as long as I wanted in that wee bit.'

There were plenty more stories and songs to pass the evening and the next day they were in the fields picking berries. My brother Henry joined them a few days later. He had been through all the homes and approved schools and was a high-spirited young man. He was a year behind Davie and at seventeen the Welfare had let him go. One of his fascinations was cars and he was always running around in some old banger. Gambling was another thing with him, and any time he had a decent bit of money you'd find him in Fife playing pitch and toss with the miners. He had a young tinker girl with him but she never had much to say. They had a couple of weeks at the berries, then got fed up, and piled into Henry's old van to head back to Dundee.

Mary invited Henry and his girlfriend along to the Gospel Mission but they had no real interest and only went for the free soup. Henry had started drinking but respected his mother's wishes and never drank in the house. After a week or so he pushed off. And not long after that Davie disappeared as well.

Then, one night, there was a knock at the door.

'Mrs Reid?' It was the police.

'Aye, what do you want?'

'It's about your son Davie.'

'What about him – is he in some kind of trouble?'

'When did you last see your son, Mrs Reid?'

'He's been away for over a week now, but that's nothing unusual. He's likely gone off with his brother or some of his pals.'

'Can you get your coat and come with us.'

'Are you lifting me?'

'No, but we need you to come down to the mortuary.'

'The morgue – what the hell do you want me to come to the morgue for?'

'We think your son Davie may have been killed.'

When she got there she found that it was Davie and that he had been electrocuted. He was always messing about in derelict buildings, collecting bits of copper and anything else that could be salvaged and turned into ready cash, and they thought he'd accidentally taken hold of a live wire. My mother never believed this for a minute, for she knew that her son knew every bit of the old buildings, and she thought it was other tinkers that threw him onto the live wire and murdered him. It was a bitter blow for her.

After Davie's death, Mary spent more time at the Gospel Mission and on the 6th September 1959 she was baptized by the Rev William Webb in the Dundee Public Baths. The Gypsy Mission then wrote a letter on her behalf to the Welfare and she was full of hope.

For me, the only thing better about the summer was the weather. It was still the same place with the same people and that man had some strange ideas about what to do with bairns during the school summer holidays. He would have you put on old coats and make you run round and round the cottage until you were sweating like a pig. He would sit on the front step reading a book and, if you stopped, or didn't run fast enough, you got a good kick up the arse from him.

The girls never had to do this. Their job was to clean the cottage top to bottom. The stone kitchen floor needed scrubbing, the walls were washed down, the linoleum was polished, and the clothes all boiled in a big china sink.

One time my sister lost a kirby grip for her hair and got a thousand lines for it. A thousand lines at seven years of age! My foster father would count every single line, and if she was even one line short, she would have to write them out all over again.

Another thing my foster father liked to do was hold a kangaroo court and that was meant to be a bit of a game. He would pretend to be a judge, and if my sister or I had done anything wrong we would be put before him. There were a few things that you could get for a punishment – maybe you would be lucky and just get a few slaps round the ear – but you never really knew what was going to happen. I lost count the number of times he threatened to put me back to the children's home and keep my sister at Balcarres with them. But I think he just said that to frighten me.

One thing that he did to Maggie will remain forever in my mind. I have no idea to this day what it was for, but nothing Maggie could have done deserved the punishment that my foster father decided to mete out to her. One very cold dark winter's night he ordered Maggie to strip down to her underwear. Wearing only a thin pair of blue cotton pants she was taken outside and made to stand barefoot facing the living room window. I was then ordered to face the same window from the comfort and warmth of the living room.

I could clearly see Maggie, on the other side of the glass, standing outside in the freezing cold. My foster father then took his seat by the fire and picked up his newspaper. He took off his boots and stretched his feet out in front the fire, then started to read. At first Maggie smiled at me through the glass and I smiled back. But, as the minutes passed I could see that my sister was starting to suffer and she started to rub her bare arms and chest with her hands. The longer she stood outside, the more vigorous the rubbing became, and she must have been absolutely freezing. When she noticed the look of concern on my face she started to pull silly faces in a pathetic attempt to cheer me up. The tears streamed down my face as she hopped from foot to foot and rubbed her body all over in her desperate efforts to keep warm. But, despite her discomfort, her main concern, as always, was to keep me from becoming too upset at the cruel punishment she was having to endure. To this day I still have a vivid picture of Maggie's chattering teeth and her sad pathetic smile.

One day my foster parents went off to Kirkcaldy and took their own bairns with them leaving me and Maggie to ourselves. We were just messing about near the cottage and seeing what we could get up to for entertainment when Maggie decides that we'll have a wander through the woods. We get deep in the woods, nobody's about and I'm sitting on a tree stump when she starts telling me more about our own people. She was going on about our mother and father, brothers and sisters, aunts and uncles, cousins etc and she remembered them all. She said our mother would come for us soon because she knew where we were after seeing her at the school. I never really gave it much thought as I had no memory of my parents and I didn't really care if they came for us or not. Maggie was my family and she was all I'd ever known. All I wished for was that our parents stayed away from the school so that Maggie wouldn't get into any more trouble if they turned up again.

If Maggie thought I wasn't listening properly she would get a bit agitated and force me to listen to her. She certainly took family matters very seriously and she was determined that I would know everything there was to know about my family and their way of life.

Just then, I spy a wee hole in the ground and see a wasp

going into it. I'm bored with her rants and make my way over to a tree where I snap a good stick. Then I'm back to the hole and poking the stick in.

'What's that you're doing Sandy?' Maggie shouts to me.

I never answered, so she comes to have a look.

'Are you mad? That's a wasps' nest you have there – keep back from it or you'll be stung to death!'

I never heeded what she was saying and gave it a few more pokes. Still nothing happened so I got a bit more aggressive and gave it a good stamp with my foot. Jings that did the trick and the wasps were out that nest raging! There were hundreds of them, all buzzing about mental.

'Oh hell!' I shout, then bolted. But my sister didn't shift fast enough and they were onto her in seconds. Her arms were flying about in the air and she was running round in circles and howling like a banshee. Well, I couldn't do anything for laughing at her antics, but when she fell over in a heap I got a bit scared and went over to her. They were crawling all over her and they were thick into her hair. I gave them a few stamps with my foot then a few whacks with my stick but that never worked and they were still on her. I tried slapping them off with my bare hands and ended up getting stung a few times. Then I panicked and ran off to get help.

I went through that wood like a hare and ran all the way to the farm, but there was nobody about, so I decided to keep going for the big house. I see Jim in a field with his tractor and shout at the top of my voice but he just waves to me and carries on. I'm in a right panic now and get myself over the dyke and start running across the field to the tractor.

'What's wrong with you son?' he says.

'The wasps have got my sister,' I shout.

'What do you mean "got your sister"?'

'The wasps,' I say. 'They're all over my sister and stinging her to bits!'

I get in the tractor with him and he puts the foot down and we're over that field in no time and belting down the dirt track. He's up and down that wood with the tractor and looking through the trees but we can't see Maggie.

'Are you sure this is where you left her Sandy?' he shouts.

'Aye, she was here,' I tell him.

He cuts the engine and listens and we hear Maggie's howls deeper in the wood. He's out of the tractor in a flash and making his way quickly through the trees and I'm right at the back of him.

When he gets to Maggie he takes off his jacket and starts swatting the wasps off her back. Then he sees that her hair's thick with them and tries picking them out with his bare hands. He lifts her and carries her quickly back to the tractor and puts the foot down again. She's moaning now and her face is all lumps and swollen. We get to the farmyard and other people arrive and they get the last of the wasps off her. I'm standing watching all this with nothing to say and a woman eventually takes me into the farmhouse. It's two weeks before I see Maggie again. I don't tell anyone how it happened but I'm miserable about it. Maggie must be hurting like hell but she doesn't say anything either.

One day they keep Maggie back off school and we're both scrubbed and put into clean clothes. My foster father tells us that the Welfare's coming to visit and we wait around all morning and it's late afternoon before the woman finally arrives.

'I've not said anything to them,' he says to her.

She tells us we're leaving this place and that's the first we know about it.

We have spent three years with this foster family and now our time in this wretched place is up.

We get in the car without any fuss and the Welfare woman drives down the dirt track. The foster folk stand at the door waving and Maggie waves back. I don't bother waving and just look out the window. We go over a cattle grid and I can see Roger walking to the big house. I knock on the window but Roger just keeps going. We get to the main road and turn right.

'This will be a new beginning for you,' the Welfare woman says.

Maggie's almost in tears now. 'What do you mean a new beginning – where are we going?'

'We have a place in a children's home for you both.'

'But we won't know anyone,' Maggie says.

'Don't worry,' continues the social worker. 'You'll make plenty of new friends in the children's home.'

I said nothing and didn't really care where we were going. I was just glad to be leaving that horrible place and to finally be rid of my cruel foster father. I could not have imagined for one minute that there could be any person, or place, worse than this in the whole world. How wrong I was. This had only been a training course. The real horrors were yet to come.

When Mary gets back to her flat in Dundee after the shops, my father's on the doorstep. He has the smell of drink on him and he asks if she's pleased to see him. He comes in and she makes him tea and he says it's a fine house she has. He likes the armchair and says it's a good carpet she has too. She says he needs to find something to do for the rest of the day as the Welfare are coming to visit and the folk from the mission will be coming as well, and it takes a ten shilling note to shift him.

My sister Helen wants back to her mum and that's why the Welfare are coming. She's been keeping a carry-on with her foster family and they've told the Welfare to take her back. She's fourteen now and the mission folk say they'll keep an eye on things and be there to help if she's allowed back to her mother.

'Have you seen your man since he got out the jail Mrs Reid?' the Welfare woman asks.

'No.'

'Will you be taking him back?'

'No.'

'We'll get Helen to you for the weekend to see if she likes you.'

'Aye.'

'And if it works out then you can have her back permanent.'

'Aye.'

In the evening, Mary's back to the mission house and after the service she's serving soup. She looks up and Henry's standing there. She fills his bowl and he sits at a table with the others. When she's finished at the counter she goes to sit with him.

'Can I have more soup Mary?' a man asks.

'Aye, help yourself,' she says.

'Stop!' It's the minister. 'You can't just help yourself to soup. Ladle it out for him Mary.'

After that the minister tells her to go and straighten the chairs in the service hall. She's busy sorting the chairs into rows when she sees a collection plate. The likes of my father never put anything in the plate, but the ones that never bothered with the soup did. There's a dose of coppers and a handful of paper notes in the collection plate and it's just the two ten shilling notes that she puts in her pocket.

When she's done, she gets her coat and Henry's waiting at the door. He starts along the street with her and the minister calls him back.

'Aye, what?'

'Away down the lodging house with the rest of them Henry. You'll get a bed there for the night. Don't be bothering Mary.'

At the weekend, Helen arrives and the Welfare don't hang

about for long. Helen tells her mum about all the places she's been in and she listens. She wants to be a nurse when she leaves the school or maybe work with animals she says and Mary tells her there's plenty jobs in the shops and factories of Dundee.

On Sunday afternoon the Welfare come back for Helen and they say she can get next weekend too if she wants to visit her mother again. Things are finally starting to look up a bit for Mary.

Greenbanks

I'm tearing along the corridor with a carrot top on my arse.

'Walk!' Matron shouts. 'How many times do you have to be told not to run along the corridor?'

I'm walking now and I can hear the lad that was chasing me uttering threats under his breath. He's a big bugger, maybe about eleven going on twelve and he's the first ginger-heided person I've seen in my life. The matron goes in her office and I'm left with him.

'Say it to my face. Go on, call me carrot top to my face!' He's raging and starts to strangle me.

'Enough!' Matron's quick out her office and puts a stop to it. We're sent to the playroom and the lad goes back to his painting. I tell my sister about him and she knocks the water jar that he dips his brushes in and it goes over his picture. That gets him raging again and we're both smirking when he's sent to sit on the bench.

If you keep a carry-on in this place it's the wooden bench outside the matron's office that you've to sit on. That way she can keep a close eye on you.

There's a dose of bairns in this place and you get them all ages from wee bairns to teenagers. And I must surely be the worst looking bairn of them all, because I'm lighter now than

I was when I arrived at my foster parents three years ago. I'm a skinny little boy with not a pick on my bones.

Greenbanks children's home was used by soldiers at the time of the war and you still have the big hospital beds on wheels in the dormitories. Maggie sleeps in the girls' dormitory and I'm in with the boys and there's strictly no talking once you're in bed and the lights are out. In the morning you're wakened by one of the staff walking up and down the dormitory swinging a hand bell. When you're up, you go to the washroom where all the windows are opened wide for fresh air and you're near frozen solid in that place. You stand on a stone floor to wash yourself at a china sink and your teeth are chattering as you try to brush them. Next you make your bed and get the dormitory cleaned up and ready for the matron's inspection. If the dormitory passes inspection you line up for breakfast and your hands and nails are checked before you get your grub.

Outside you have swings and a sand pit and a good bit of grass to run about on. This day the ginger boy has me up against the wall, but Maggie's over quick and kicks him round the park and that puts a stop to her pocket money on the Saturday afternoon. If you break the rules, raise your voice indoors, don't do what they tell you, or keep any kind of carry-on in this place, they're down on you quick. So, you've to watch yourself and pay attention to what they want you to do.

They put me to Parkhill school in Leven. There's a dose of bairns in my class but I'm the only one from the home and I've to sit and play with a bit plasticine because they think I'm behind with my lessons. I'm in primary one and the other bairns had all started school about two months before me.

The teacher's a tall woman with white hair and her name's Mrs Martin. One day I'm whistling in the class so she keeps me back at playtime. 'Where did you learn that tune you were whistling?' she says, and she tells me it was a man called

Mozart who made it up. She puts a bairn's book in front of me and asks me to read it. 'Who taught you to read?' she asks and I tell her it was my sister. 'Who told me you were backward?' she mutters to herself as she walks away.

Sometimes you're sent for a haircut after the school and it's more a pluck than a cut. The man uses a pair of hand clippers and your hair's ripped out by the roots. A boy waits for me outside and when the barber's finished we go behind the shop. We see cardboard boxes piled against the wall and this lad puts a match to them and I'm back to the home in a police car. The matron's raging and puts a stop to my pocket money on Saturday afternoon and it's the whole weekend I've to lie in bed and I'm only allowed up to go to the toilet and eat my meals. But me and that lad become good pals and sometimes we dodge the school altogether and look for more interesting things to do.

At Christmas time they put on entertainment and one night a magic man comes to show us tricks. We put out chairs and I'm in row three. He's dressed like a wizard and shouts, 'Hello boys and girls,' to us.

'Hello,' we shout back.

'I'm Roger The Dodger,' he says.

'Hello Roger The Dodger,' we roar back and that gets him started on the tricks. He turns a red ball into a blue ball then casts a spell and a bird appears in an empty cage.

'Look, a pigeon!' one of the bairns shouts and the wizard says it's a dove. He takes helpers from the front row and gives them sweets so I stand up to get the man's attention and I'm told to sit on my arse.

Some tricks are rubbish but others are good and he keeps his best trick for last when he pulls a rabbit from a top hat. He goes to the front row and lets a wee lassie stroke it and the bugger fastens onto her finger. The blood's dripping and the rabbit's on the floor running round the bairns.

'Catch that!' the matron shouts and the man's after it. Rabbits never bothered me but some of the wee bairns are upset and crying and that man's desperate to get a hold of the bugger.

'Hurry up!' the matron roars, but it keeps dodging him and the wee wizard's raging now and cursing at the rabbit. It comes near me so I grab it by the neck and hand it to the man and the matron tells him to pack up his tricks and get out the place.

On Christmas morning, every bairn has a dose of presents to wake up to and after the church service you can rip the paper off them. I get a cowboy suit with two guns and two holsters and a big box packed with adventure stuff like a compass, water bottle and plastic hunting knife and the matron says you'll be fine if you get lost like Robinson Crusoe. They pack a big Christmas dinner into you and in the afternoon the staff are put off their heads with the noise all the bairns make with their new toys. It's great. The lassies have dolls, sewing sets, colouring books and rubbish like that and it's the boys that get the better stuff.

I never thought much of the adventure pack and was out to get a swap. I near struck a deal with this lad for a robot that could walk if you wound it up with a key, but decided instead to swap with this other lad for his leather football. Later, at night, you sang hymns round the Christmas tree then that was your day over and you were packed off to your bed. It was one of the best days I could remember.

My sister could be a vicious bugger and one day she splits my lip and knocks one of my teeth out with a dinky car and that gets me raging. I'm after her with a stick and she locks herself in the staff bathroom. I'm battering at the door with the stick and the matron comes along and takes it from me. Maggie's in trouble for knocking out my tooth and that gets her early bed for a week. That's a bad thing to get because you're sent straight to bed after your tea and you can hear the other bairns running about outside while you've to lie bored in your bed.

One day I take the jaundice and that's me laid up. The bairns are at school and I'm lying in bed with nothing to do. A lassie comes in and tells me she has mumps. She's about fourteen and says it's the yellow fever I've took and that there's a good chance I'll die with it. I tell her that's rubbish and that the matron says it's jaundice I'm smitten with and all you do is turn a bit yellow for a few days and then you're fine after that.

'You ever seen a lassie's tits?' she says.

'No.'

'Want to see mine?'

'Aye.'

She opens her blouse and that's the first pair of tits I ever saw.

On Saturday morning a wee woman comes to sew your clothes and darn your socks. She's an old woman with grey hair and she sings bible songs and hands out sweets to all the bairns. If you've a mind to join in you can learn the songs but I never bothered with that and I still got the sweets from her.

In the afternoon you lined up outside the office for your pocket money and the queue went right down the corridor. It took about an hour to get your money and how much you got depended on your age. It was four-pence that I qualified for. The threepenny bit you could spend on sweets, but the penny you had to hold back for the Sunday morning and the church collection plate. God help you if you tried to hold your donation back, for the matron kept a close eye on the whole thing and the last bairn handed the plate to her and she would count every penny before handing it on to one of the church men.

The place also had a boiler man to keep the pipes working and it was his job to fix anything else that was broken. He was a wee fat man with a bald head and thick glasses and he never bothered with a tool box just carried a hammer about with him. He could fix anything from a television set to a broken wheel on your cartie with that hammer. He told me you needed to know whether to give something two or three taps or just the one big whack. He was a bit of a magic man as well and if you went to see him in his boiler room he would put on a wee show for you with coins and a pack of cards that he always had handy.

One day, when we're settled down in the place, a new boy arrives. His nose is smashed and you'd think he'd been slapped with a frying pan.

'What's wrong with your face?' I say.

'There's nothing wrong with my face,' he says.

'How did you get that?'

'Get what?' he says, and I think maybe he's a bit daft, so I never bothered with any more questions for him.

It turns out the lad's fine and he has a harelip so I take him to meet my sister. We pass the matron on the way outside and she says, 'Is that a new friend you have there Sandy?' and I tell her I'm only trying the lad out.

We're outside and my sister meets him.

'What happened to your face?' she says.

'There's nothing wrong with my face,' he says.

'How's it like that?'

'Like what?' he says.

I wink to my sister. 'His face is just fine Maggie. The next time someone asks what's wrong with your face just you tell them to fuck off!'

The ginger boy's drawing pictures on the wall with chalk and I take the lad over to meet him. 'Have you met the new boy?' I say.

'What happened to your face?' Ginger asks.

'Fuck off!' the lad says, and Ginger puts him on his arse

with one punch and that's me and her laughing when he runs away crying.

On a Sunday you're put to the church. We all line up and the matron checks to see that everyone has their penny for the collection plate then you're marched up the street in your Sunday best. The minister at Scoonie Church could talk for fun and you'd to listen to that man until half time when they let you out for the Sunday school.

Sunday school was better than the church and you got good stories from the teachers about bible men like Moses and the disciples. But my favourite man was Samson who tore down buildings with his bare hands when he was raging. Two women taught you a dose of Christian songs and they had a prize for the bairn who could draw the best picture of Jesus.

Sunday dinner was the best of the week and you got roast beef with tatties and Brussels sprouts. Some of the bairns never liked vegetables and the matron would be on to them to clean their plate but I was fine with my grub and would eat anything they put down for me bar potted hoch.

In the afternoon you were out of your Sunday best and back into your play clothes for a walk to Letham Glen. I liked this place for you had a burn and a dose of trees and grass to run about on and it was just like you were back in the countryside. They just let you run wild in this place and never bothered if you roared and ran about like madmen.

It was a fifteen-minute walk from the home to the school and that meant it would take me about an hour. I just mucked about and would never be anywhere near the place when the bell went. When they complained about my lateness the matron packed me off early before the other bairns, but it made no difference and I was still late for my lessons.

My teacher took a shine to me and said if I kept quiet in the classroom and stuck in at my lessons she would ask the home if she could have me back to her house for my tea sometime.

Then, one day, an Action Man went missing from some lad's schoolbag and the headmaster had the police in the school to investigate the disappearance. It was the same policeman that got me for the fire behind the barber shop and he told me that he'd had enough of the carry-on I keep. He said that he knew my father and that he was a thief and that he suspected I was a thief too. He thinks I took the Action Man and tells me to own up to stealing it. I tell him I was never near the lad's schoolbag and that I had nothing to do with the Action Man going missing. He says he thinks it was me that took it and says he'll be keeping a close eye on me in the future. And if I come to his attention again I'll be put to an approved school where they know just how to handle bad little buggers like me.

We've been in the place for about a year and a half now and one day they hold Maggie and me back from the school. The matron tells us that the Welfare has found another foster home for us and that we're to be shipped out the place. There's nothing you can do about that and you don't get to choose whether or not to go. So I just hope it's going to be better than the last place.

'Did you sleep well lassie?'

'Aye, it's a rare comfy bed you have there Ma.'

'Get yourself up and come through to the living room, I've a drop tea waiting for you.'

Helen sits next to her mother at the fire. 'Drink your tea lassie.'

'I don't like tea, it's milk I usually get.'

'You're better to try tea – it warms your bones in the morning lassie.'

They talk more and Mary tells Helen about her brothers and sisters. 'Have you seen any of them in the homes you've been through Helen?'

'I've never seen a soul Ma. I wouldn't know a brother or sister if they were standing right next to me.'

'Aye, well, you've a brother Davie that died no long ago.'

'Died Ma?'

'Aye, he was electrocuted in an old building just up the road from here.'

'What age was he when that happened?'

'Eighteen, lass. He was biding here with me at the time.'

'You must miss him Ma?'

'Aye, he's lying in the Eastern Cemetery, God rest him.'

Helen washed her face then they went to the shop. On the way back they see some rough looking men drinking on waste ground. They're keeping a right carry-on and Mary takes her daughter's arm and crosses the street.

'Are they tinkers Ma?'

'Aye.'

'Do you know them Ma?'

'Aye.'

'Who are they Ma?'

'Just some wild buggers that's no worth bothering about lassie.'

Suddenly all hell erupts and the men start kicking the brains out each other. Helen takes her mother's hand for the first time. 'Maybe you should tell a policeman Ma?'

'No, they're fine. Best just to leave them to it.' Mary did not mention to Helen that her father was one of the men.

Saturday night's a busy night at the mission house and Helen helps her mother to dish out the soup after the service. There's a right carry-on at the door and some of the men are arguing with the minister.

'Can we come in for some soup?' one of them shouts.

'No you can't! And you can get away from this door or I'll have the police onto the lot of you,' the minister shouts.

'Why are they not getting in Ma?'

'My, you're a bonny lassie,' Tommy Henderson says.

'Aye, she's one of my bairns,' says Mary.

'That's an awful carry-on your man's keeping at the door Mary,' he says.

'My man's no with that lot,' she says, and gives Tommy a look.

'Aye, he's there Mary. Blind drunk – and roaring at the minister!'

'Do you want soup or not Tommy Henderson?'

'Aye.'

'Well shut your face and see that bowl from you!'

When they get back to the house Mary pokes the fire and throws on some coal and before long they have a good blaze going.

'What a braw heat. I love an open fire Ma,' Helen says.

'Do you not have a fire in the home?'

'No, but my foster place had one. It's just pipes you have in the home Ma, and they're always freezing cold.'

'Pull your seat in and get a good heat lassie and you can tell me more about yourself.'

Helen tells her that she likes to listen to pop songs but most of the records that they have in the home are scratched and you can't hear them right. Mary says that she has some money put aside and that she'll buy some records for her soon.

'Why did they take me away from you Ma?'

'We lived in a tent and it was a house you needed to raise bairns in according to the Welfare.'

'Were you raised in a tent Ma?'

'Aye.'

'Did the Welfare take you away when you were a bairn?'

'No.'

'How no?'

'It was different then. It was just after the First War and they had no interest in taking bairns and putting them into homes then.'

'Was my daddy in the war Ma?'

'Aye, for about a fortnight. Then he buggered off and took to the hills.'

'Did he?'

'Aye, it was the Second War they wanted him for.'

'Was it?'

'Aye, and me and your granny had to keep him going in grub.'

'Drink as well Ma?' Helen laughed.

'Aye, he likes a good drink your father, but he never got much of the stuff when he was up in the hills.'

'Do you drink Ma?'

'I'm stone sober and a Christian. I wouldn't put a drink to my mouth!'

'But did you drink before Ma?'

'Aye.'

'Is that how they took all your bairns away Ma?'

'Och, they never needed much of a reason to take tinker bairns away from their families Helen.'

'What do you mean Ma?'

'If you were different from other folk, supposing you lived in a camp, instead of a house, that would be enough for the Welfare to take your bairns away lassie.'

'That's terrible Ma.'

'Aye, we were different, and they wanted us all to come out the camps and move into houses like the rest of them. They never liked tinkers going about you see. And they wanted to put a stop to our way of life. They thought if they could get the bairns away from us then they would grow up differently and eventually forget all about their own families and their way of life. They wanted to wipe us out!'

'Wipe us out Ma!'

'Aye, and if that man Hitler had won the war it would have been worse!'

'Worse?'

'Aye, he would have put the lot of us into a room and turned on the gas tap!'

'Kill us?'

'Aye!'

'He wouldn't be allowed to do that Ma.'

'No, and the Welfare were no allowed to do that either – so it was the homes they put our bairns in.'

'How many bairns did you have?'

'There's a dozen of you – twelve altogether.'

'That's a lot of bairns Ma!'

'Aye, the first born was a wee laddie but he died at two weeks. Then I had your brother Davie and he was electrocuted. It was seven laddies and four lassies I had. So you've a dose of brothers and sisters still to meet!'

There was a silence before Helen spoke again. 'Did you miss me Ma?'

'Of course I missed you lassie! I miss every one of my bairns.'

They laughed and Helen asked more questions about her brothers and sisters. She held her mother's hand now. 'I like you Ma, and I'm going to ask the Welfare if I can stay with you permanent.'

Mary chuckled. 'Don't build your hopes up there lassie – they're strange people the Welfare!'

'If they don't let me stay with you I'll run away.'

Mary smiled. 'Aye, no doubt you would. Now, it's time for your bed lassie.'

It was close to midday when they were wakened by Henry banging at the front door.

'What do you want Henry?'

'Were you still in your bed Mary?'

'Aye, now if it's money you're after – I've none!'

'You must have something woman – I'm choking for a drink!'

'You'll be choking with my hands round your neck if you don't get away from this door right now Henry Reid!'

'Ten shillings and I'll be off Mary.'

'I've told you, I've nothing to give you Henry!'

'You must have something Mary.'

She goes to the kitchen for her purse and he's in the living room by the time she's back. 'You'll be the death of me man,' she says, handing him five shillings.

Helen comes through. 'Is that my father Ma?'

'Aye – pay him no heed.'

'Which one are you?' he says.

'Do you not know your own lassie Henry Reid? It's Helen, she's here for the weekend and she'll be going back to the home later today.'

'Aye, can you make it ten shillings Mary?' He showed little interest in Helen – it was just drink he was after.

'I've no more money Henry – now bugger off!'

'Do they give you pocket money in that place Helen?' he asked.

'You leave that lassie alone!' Mary hissed.

'Just a wee bit more and I'll be out your hair woman!'

She's back in her purse and hands him another half crown. 'That's all I can give you Henry. I've got records to buy for Helen.'

'Records! What the hell do you want with records – you don't have a record player!'

'Are you deaf? I said they're for Helen!'

He snatches her purse. 'Records my arse!'

She snatches it back and he lands a punch in her face. Next he's got her by the hair and Helen's out the door in a flash. By the time she comes back with a policeman her father's gone and the place is in bits.

'Do you want him lifted?' the policeman asks.

'I'm fine,' Mary says. Her daughter has a wet cloth to her swollen face. 'Look at the place Helen – it's in bits.'

'Never mind about that Ma.'

'Every ornament, every single dish – the bastard's even put the windows in!'

'Do you want him lifted?' the policeman asks again.

'That man fucks me up – I can't do anything for him!'

The Welfare woman comes through the door and talks with the policeman.

'They'll no let you back now Helen,' Mary whispers.

'They can't stop me Ma.'

'Helen, come here,' the Welfare woman says.

Mary squeezes her daughter's hand. 'I'm sorry lass.'

'Helen!'

'You better go now lass.'

'I don't want to leave you Ma.'

'I'll be fine.' She manages a smile.

'Look at your face Ma.'

'Never mind my face.'

'Come on Helen, we need to be going now.' The Welfare woman's becoming impatient.

Mary presses a ten shilling note into Helen's hand. 'Get your records lassie.'

'I'll see you next week Ma.'

'Aye.'

'They'll not keep me from you Ma.'

If you've ever seen a giraffe then you've an idea how high this man stood. He's a beanpole with a Hitler moustache and she's a wee fat woman with a bun in her hair. We're only a week in the place and I think that's them sick of us. 'Don't do this, don't do that, watch my ornaments, wipe your feet, stop your swearing . . .' She's never off our backs, and she's never without the knitting pins under her arms.

It's a feast then a fast in this place and it's him that cooks, but only when she wants to eat. He does what she says and all she does is bleat.

'I don't know why we bothered,' she says, and he nods. 'Of all the bairns needing good homes, it's that two that we get, and they'll put me clean off my head with the noise they make!'

He tells me to shut up and puts his rolled newspaper round my lug. It's the thick glasses he has and the thick glasses she has too. My sister says we were better in the home. We've to share a bed in this place and I'm sick of her pishing it every night.

It's Kirkcaldy we're in and the house sits in a street with a dose of other houses and there's plenty bairns that you can play with.

'If I look out the window and you're not in sight – that's you two in for good!' the woman says.

One day we're out playing and Maggie says, 'That man feels my arse all the time.'

'He never feels mine,' I say.

'That's because you're a laddie,' she says.

There's a lad with a caliper on each leg and he's about the same age as me and wants to be my pal. Maggie says not to bother with him because he's a cripple and nobody likes cripples that much. She says no one ever plays with him so pay him no heed and don't be bothering much with him.

One day we're through all the streets of Kirkcaldy and eventually come to a fair. There's big fancy rides and a dose of bairns run about screaming and shouting with the excitement of the place.

'Do you want to try for a coconut?' a man shouts to Maggie.

'What's a coconut?'

'One of them,' he says, pointing to the row of coconuts behind him.

'What do you have to do?'

'Knock one off,' he says, holding three rubber balls out to her.

'And then it belongs to you?'

'Yes, that's all there is to it. Knock one over and it's yours to keep!'

'Aye ok, see the balls from you.'

The man holds back. 'Wait a minute now lass, have you a penny?'

'No,' she says.

'Well that's a pity because you need a penny to try for a coconut.'

'Bugger!'

We're just about to go away when a man puts a penny in my sister's hand and tells her to have a shot. I ask the man for a penny too and she tells me to shut up and not to be so greedy. She throws the three balls squint and that wins us bugger all. The man says he'll give it a go and knocks one clean off its perch with the very first ball he throws. He never bothers with the other two balls and hands them to me. But I'm no use and miss them like she did. The showman hands over the coconut and Maggie gets it.

'What do you do with it?' she asks.

'You eat it.'

'How do you eat it?'

'You've to open it first.'

'Burst it you mean?'

'Yes.'

Maggie stots it off the ground a few times but it won't break and the man says we can get it open later. This man would do anything you asked him to do and he pays for any rides we want to try out. Maggie's fed up with the coconut now and

I'm left to carry it. We come to a strong man's challenge where you've to smack a steel plate with a big sledgehammer and there's a prize if you can make a bell ring at the top. A few big lads have had a go but none of them got the bell to ring and they're no use. Maggie asks our new friend to have a go, but he says he never bothers with things like that and just likes to watch.

A man comes along and he's a giant of a man with great big muscles and he looks the type to make that bell ring. He hands his money over and takes off his jacket. He lifts the hammer right over his head and gives out a mighty roar, but before that hammer strikes I have the coconut on the steel plate and that's it smashed!

Me and her are having a rare time at this fair and things are just fine. We go from one ride to the next and the man just pays for any ride you want to try out until a policeman comes along and puts a stop to it.

'What are you doing with these bairns Michael?'

'I'm putting them on the rides to give them some enjoyment,' he says.

'Aye, well I think they've had quite enough enjoyment for one day. Now away home with you and don't let me see you wandering about the fair again.'

The man doesn't need telling twice and away he goes.

'What's your name?' the policeman asks me.

'Sandy.'

'Sandy what?'

'Sandy Reid.'

'What age are you Sandy?'

'I'm nearly seven.'

'What's your name?' he asks her.

'Maggie.'

'Maggie what?'

'Maggie Reid.'

'You're brother and sister?'

'Aye.'

'And where do you live?'

'I'm no sure,' Maggie says.

'You're not sure, you don't know where you stay?'

'We've just landed in the place.'

'What do you mean just landed in the place?'

'It's a foster home we're in.'

'I see. And you can't remember where your foster home is?'

'No.'

'Alright,' he says. 'You can come with me and I'll find out who your foster folk are and get you back to them.'

We've only been a few weeks with the people and that's them finished with us now. Disappearing off to the fair and being delivered home by the police is too much for them to cope with.

'They put me off my head with worry. They won't do a thing I tell them and they swear like troopers. I don't think they like me and I don't think they like him. So, there's not much point in keeping them here. You'll have to take them back to the home!'

The Welfare have no choice but I'm pleased we don't have to stay with Mr Giraffe and his miserable missus.

The first night back in Greenbanks all the bairns have to sit through a slide show with pictures about bairns out in Africa that are starving and don't have food like we do. The matron tells us we're very lucky to be in a children's home where we have good food and a warm bed to sleep in every night. The African bairns have to live in refugee camps and sleep outside in tents. She says there's others yet that have to lie in mud huts because they don't have enough tents to go round them all. She says we've got a cheek to moan about a drop rain when the wee black bairns are baked by the sun that's so hot it cooks their brains. Some of the collection at the church gets shipped to them she says. And missionaries are there to hand out food. One wee lad says that the African bairns are fatter than any of us and she tells him that's because their bellies are swollen with the hunger.

We slept in tents, my sister says when she gets me on my own. And there were no missionaries waiting outside our camp to put grub in our bellies. She tells me to pay no heed to the African bairns.

There are new faces in the place and some of the bairns I knew before have been boarded out or gone home. The ginger boy's still here and one afternoon he comes over to see what I'm drawing.

'What's that?' he asks.

'A picture.'

'I know it's a picture. But what's it supposed to be?'

'Are you blind? It's a wood with trees and that's a field with neeps at the bottom and that's the sky at the top.'

'Bring it over to my table,' he says.

He takes his brush and puts green paint where the field is and starts to colour in the trees. He takes his time and makes a good job. He puts blue paint for the sky and I tell him to make it a red sky, like a good summer's night and to do some of the trees a different colour too. He gets fed up with my demands and puts his paintbrush down. He tells me to go and draw the picture again and to paint it myself.

A lad arrives in the place and all he can do is bang his head on the pillow and make gurgling noises like a baby. And he does this the whole night long. Me and a few other lads tell him to shut up but he pays no heed and even in his sleep that lad roars like a banshee with the bad dreams that he's having. I report him to the matron in the morning and she says to ignore him and to stick my fingers in my lugs. That way you won't hear him ranting and you'll get a good night's sleep she says.

When the summer comes you get taken to St Andrews for your summer holidays. The home takes a dose of caravans from the man that has the site at Kinkell Braes and what a view you have over the sea from this site and you can see the big ships further out and the wee ships further in. The place looks over St Andrews Bay and you have people from Glasgow and people from Perth and people from Inverness. And they come here from a heap of towns down in England as well.

All the bairns are down to the beach every single day and the only thing I don't like about it is the plastic sandals you've to wear on your two feet. You can paddle in the sea or look in rock pools for crabs and if you're lucky you'll maybe land a wee fish in your net. There's a dose of bairns and dogs running about the place and everyone's enjoying their summer holidays. There's lots to do and it's good to get a change.

When I go for a sandwich I ask the matron if I can leave off the plastic sandals because they nip my feet but she says to keep them on in case I put my foot on a bit glass or something else that can tear me.

We crowd round an ice cream van and it's the younger bairns that get served first and the older bairns have to wait longer for their cones. By the time my sister gets hers I'm finished mine and it takes the man about an hour to dish out all the cones to the bairns from Greenbanks.

'Will you be back tomorrow?' he asks the matron.

'We'll be here for a week,' she tells him.

'That's fine by me,' he says. 'I'll be here every day waiting to serve you.'

The matron picks out all the bairns she wants to keep a close eye on and that means I'm in her caravan for the week. There are gas mantles you light at night and you can see just the same with them as you could with an electric light bulb but the matron says she can't make out her book with them and that they're useless. When you're packed off to bed it's the same rules here as you have in the home and that means no talking in your bed.

One day we go on a trip to Dundee and we're let loose in a shop to pick any toy you like. After that you're taken for high tea at a fancy restaurant, then it's off to the theatre in the evening where the seats have been booked for us in advance. The show we're going to see is the matron's favourite and that's called An Evening with Tom and Jack, the Alexander Brothers.

We take up the front and half the second row and we're all waiting to be entertained. It's a man and woman you have on the stage first to warm you up and I think they're rubbish and tell the matron and she says the Alexander Brothers will be much better when they come on.

When the lights go down for the second time we're told to keep quiet and when a lad farts we're all in fits of laughter and that gets the matron raging and she threatens to take us all out the place and straight back to St Andrews. The curtain opens and the Alexander brothers are on the stage in their kilts and I sit back to see what these lads can do. And what a show they put on for us. They have much better jokes than the pair that were on before them and I know half their songs, because the matron plays them in the home, and they have you in stitches when they sing a song the way an old woman would sing it.

About halfway through the show one of the lads comes to the front and tells me to stand up. 'What's your name?' he asks.

'Sandy Reid,' I tell him.

'Sandy – that's short for Alexander,' he says.

'Aye.'

'Well that makes you one of the Alexander Brothers!' he shouts, and tells me to come up on the stage to help them out with the show.

I'm up on the stage and trying to make out the other bairns and staff but I can hardly see anything for the spotlight they have shining in my eyes.

'Do you know who I am Sandy?' one of the lads asks me.

'Tom?'

'No, no – he's Tom!' he says laughing, and points to the other lad. 'And I'm Jack.'

Tom comes over and shakes my hand and that gets the crowd roaring.

'Now Sandy,' he says. 'Have you ever worn a kilt?'

'No.'

'You're telling me you're a Scotsman but you've never worn a kilt!' The crowd roars again when Tom puts a tartan rug round my waist.

'You have a kilt now,' he says. 'So all we need now is a wee song from you. Do you know any good Scottish songs?'

'Aye.'

'Would you like to sing your wee song to all the people out there?'

'Aye, I will.'

'Right, let's have a big hand for Sandy Reid,' he shouts, and they all clap. Then I sing my song.

Skinny Malinky long legs, umbrella feet
Went to the pictures and could'na find a seat
When the pictures started Skinny Malinky farted . . .

A man grabs my arm and gets me quickly to the side. He whips the bit tartan off my waist and tells me to go and sit on my arse and Tom and Jack carry on the show without me. The lads keep their biggest hit for last and it's just the one spotlight they have shining on them when they sing 'I'm Nobody's Child' to a dose of bairns from a children's home.

* * *

'Mary! Is that you?'

'Aye, it's me Sandy and my feet are killing me.'

'Have you come all the way from Dundee?'

'Aye.'

'That's a good walk for you.'

'How are you Mary?' It was Peggy and she gives a smile.

'I'm fine Peggy, a bit weary, but fine.'

'I hear your man's in Kirkcaldy,' Sandy says.

'Aye, he'll no show his face round me in a hurry – that man put my house in bits!'

'Bastard!' Peggy says.

Mary sits and Sandy throws a few sticks on the fire. He has a good blaze going and Peggy makes tea. She hands a mug to Mary and Sandy takes his in a jam jar for it's only the two mugs that Peggy has.

Mary tells them about Helen visiting and how things had gone so well until Henry spoiled everything and they listened to her story. Peggy says Mary's brain is flooded with worry over her bairns and the death of Davie and Sandy agrees.

'Away in the tent and get your head down,' Peggy says.

My older brother did really well at the pitch and toss and came away with a good bundle of notes in his pocket.

'How much do you have there Henry?' It was his pal Billy.

'Over two hundred quid.'

'You couldn't put a foot wrong Henry.'

'Aye, I was sore due that win Billy and I'm going to celebrate.'

They get in Henry's old motor and drive to Kirkcaldy where they find a pub. Today was a good day and Henry's determined that it will be a good night too as he starts to knock back the whisky.

An old miner says, 'I hear you had some good luck today Henry.'

'Aye, do you want a drink?'

'That's kind of you Henry. I'll have a whisky if you don't mind.'

Henry orders the drink and the old man says, 'There was a man in the bar a couple of days back and he had a racing dog with him.'

'Did he?'

'Aye, and it was the best looking greyhound you ever saw in your life. Now, while that man's drinking his beer, the dog goes behind the bar and helps itself to a whole tray of pies!'

'Greedy bugger.'

'Aye, but listen to this. The dog was meant to be racing that night and just about the whole town of Kirkcaldy had money running on the thing.'

'Did you have money on too?'

'Aye I had money on. It was a fast dog and favourite to win its race.'

'What happened?'

'When the time came to race it could barely get out the traps with the pies that were into it and it came last out the lot of them!'

'Bugger!'

'Aye, and it left me skint!'

'Did you have a good skelp on it?'

'Everything! I had every penny that belonged me riding on that dog!'

'And a dose of people lost money on that dog I suppose?'

'Aye.'

'And no one saw it eat all the pies?'

'Just me.'

'Another three whiskies barman.'

'You're a gentleman Henry Reid.'

'Aye, now take your whisky and bugger off! Away and tell your doggy story to someone else.'

At closing time the pair of them are well scunnered.

'I'll drive,' Henry says, fumbling in his pockets for the keys to the old motor.

'If you can find your keys, I'd be better to drive Henry.'

'Bugger off, you're more drunk than me Billy.'

They're halfway to Sandy's camp when Henry puts the car in a ditch.

'For fuck sake Henry. I said I would be better driving!'

Henry hands Billy the keys and after a struggle they manage to get the motor out the ditch and back onto the road. He falls asleep and Billy tries to waken him for directions to Sandy's camp. His eyes are off the road for a split second and that's them whacked into a tree. This time the old motor's knackered and they get out to walk.

The next day brings a fine morning and Sandy has a good fire going before the two women are up. Then he sees a police car pull up beside the wood.

'That's the Hornies [police],' he shouts.

'Are they coming to the tent?' Peggy asks.

'Aye.'

'I wonder what they want?' Mary says, and gets up with Peggy to join Sandy outside.

'Hello Sandy,' the policeman says.

'Hello Constable. What brings you out here?'

'I'm looking for your nephew.'

'Which one? I've got a dose of nephews.'

'Young Henry. The lad that's always running about in cars.'

'That's my laddie,' Mary says.

'You're his mother?'

'Aye.'

'Well he's crashed his motor and I need to get a grip of him.'

'Is he alright?'

'Aye, well enough to walk away. But I'll need to put some questions to him.'

Mary went back in the tent and Peggy followed.

'That laddie of yours will come to grief one day in a motor car if he's no careful Mary.'

'Aye, I'll need to have a word with him about that Peggy.'

After your summer holiday you've to get yourself ready for the seaside mission because that's what's coming next. The matron's forever telling me to be on my best behaviour or when the mission comes I'll not be seeing it and that would mean I'm left behind and she says I wouldn't like that and neither would she.

I'm not on the best of terms with my sister and me and her's been at each other's throats a lot lately, and it's more her at mine than me at hers. She has a white rabbit she keeps in a cage outside and she never bothers much with me nowadays and it's the rabbit that gets her attention and I'm left to muck about by myself. 'You can play with some of the other lads,' she says, but I never really bother much with them and it's her that I want to play with.

I'm outside and looking at this rabbit in its cage and decide that it's either him or me and that one of us needs to go. I open the cage and get him by the neck. I'm over to the wall and drop him down on the grass at the other side. 'Bugger off,' I shout, but it just sits there eating the grass. A wee lad comes up the street and he's about the same age as me and asks if I want my rabbit back and I tell him to bugger off too. He just stands looking at the rabbit, so I tell him again and this time he shouts back, 'You're in the home for bad boys' and I tell him he's right and that I'm the worst one of the lot and if he doesn't bugger off right now I'll come over that wall and kick his fucking arse. He starts to get impudent with me so I fire a couple of stones at him and that gets him running up the street crying.

My attention's back to the rabbit now and it's still grazing. I jump over the wall and grab it then I cross the road and start up the street. You're not meant to be out the place and this can get you in big trouble but I don't bother with that and just keep going with this rabbit in my arms and it's a street further on before I toss it in a garden where there's a bit grass.

A woman passes and she says, 'What are you doing out the home wee boy?' and threatens to tell the matron that I'm out the place but I don't bother with her and wander off to see what there is to do.

I'm at the station and look to see if there's any trains going about. I go through a gate and cross the track. Then I'm through another gate on the other side. Past the railway you have a big yard where I've mucked about before and I know for a fact there's plenty you can get up to here.

I see a crate of empty milk bottles outside the place where the railwaymen take their tea. I start to smash the bottles off a wall and there's bits of glass flying in all directions and I'm having fun until a man puts a stop to it. 'Get away out the yard you wee bugger,' he roars. I pay him no heed and go up close to the wall to smash the last bottle. I let fly, and a bit of glass takes a chunk out my leg, just below my knee cap.

The blood's running down my leg and my sock's covered in blood. I decide it's time for me to get myself back to the home and I'm back over the railway line when a man and woman stop me. 'What happened to your leg wee boy?' she says. 'And look at the blood coming out that laddie's leg!' He says, 'That boy's from the Greenbanks home and we'd better take him back.'

The matron gets the doctor out and he puts a big needle straight in the cut and that was sore. He sews me up with a needle and thread and that's me fixed. The matron says that's what happens when you go out the place on your own and she tells me never to do that again.

It's the next day before Maggie notices the rabbit's away

and she's raging. With the cage door open the matron thinks maybe some lads from outside came in the grounds and stole the rabbit. I never said a word about the thing until the next time me and her's at it. Then I told her that I let the bugger loose. When I see how upset she is, I feel sorry for getting rid of the rabbit but maybe when she's calmed down she'll pay me a bit more attention.

One night the matron comes into the playroom with a policeman and she lines us all up to listen to what this bobby has to say. It's the same bobby that got me for the fire and the same bobby that got me for the Action Man and the same bobby that's taken a dislike to me. He says that money's gone missing from the office and that it's a good bit of money and that he thinks it's an inside job. 'Someone in this room has pinched that money and I'll get to the bottom of it!' he says.

He tells everyone to turn out their pockets. Nobody has any money and that's his enquiries at a standstill. 'I know this lad,' he says, looking at me. 'And I know that if anyone pinched that money it would likely be him.' He pokes a finger in my chest and says to remember that he's keeping a close eye on me and that he'll be there when I step out of line. When he leaves the crime's still unsolved.

A short time later, the matron says to me, 'Sandy, you need a club to go to,' and it's the Lifeboys she picks for me. She takes me in the van down to the hut where the Lifeboys meet on a Tuesday night and leaves me with the man that runs the place.

'I'm going to show you how to tie a knot,' he says to me.

'Aye, Captain.'

'Have you tied a knot before Sandy?'

'Aye, Captain,' I say, and point to my shoe laces.

'That's not that type of knot I mean laddie. I'm going to teach you how to tie a different kind of knot.'

'Aye, Captain.'

'It's a knot that would be useful to a sailor.'

'Aye, Captain.'

'Will you stop calling me Captain all the time – my name's Mr Bennet!'

'Aye, Mr Bennet.'

'Now do you want to learn how to tie this knot or not?'

'Aye, Mr Bennet.'

'Here's a bit rope.'

'Thank you, Mr Bennet.'

'Now watch closely and do exactly what I do with my rope.'

'Aye, Mr Bennet.'

'Will you stop calling me Mr Bennet all the time laddie!'

'What do you want me to call you?'

'Look I'll show you how to tie the knot some other time.' He's fed up with me already and goes to teach the sailor's knot to some other boys.

Some of the lads can tie some right fancy knots and they have badges to prove it. I ask this lad what you've to do to get a dose of badges like the ones he has sewn on his jacket and he says you've to learn to tie good knots first, then the man tests you and if you pass the test then you'll get a knot badge. They all have a sailor's hat on their heads and I want one too.

'Mr Bennet?'

'What is it laddie?'

'Have you a sailor's hat that would do me?'

'Any hat you get you've to buy,' he says.

'How much is a sailor's hat?'

'Never you mind about the price laddie. If you stick with the Lifeboys the matron will buy a hat for you.'

'Have you a spare hat that I can try out?' I ask, and he says he'll have a look.

I'm back with the other lad now and he's showing me how to tie a different knot. I'm busy working it out when the man's back with a sailor's hat for me to try. This hat's miles too big and must have come off a boy with a much bigger head than me.

I went back to the Lifeboys a few more times, then I got fed up with it and asked the matron to find a better club for me where more happens.

There seems to be something going on with the people outside and more and more bairns are landing in the children's home. You can see new faces all the time and if you're unlucky you can end up with a boy that snores like a pig lying in the bed next to you in the dormitory. The matron's going off her head with the amount of bairns in the place and the carry-on that they all keep.

When the Sunday school picnic comes round it's a big yellow bus they have to take us all to Craigtoun Park where we join up with all the other bairns from the Sunday school. The staff handed out streamers to hang out the bus windows and when we got started with the singing, what a racket we made, and the staff and matron were put clean off their heads by the time we got to that park.

There was just about everything in the world to do at this park and the first thing I made for was the putting. I got a golf club and when the man handed me a golf ball he said. 'If you lose it the home will be charged for another one.'

There's a dose of bairns playing at the putting and once you're finished with a hole you've to wait ages before you can get playing the next one. I get fed up waiting around so go off to find something more interesting to do. There's another golf game you can try in this park and that's called crazy golf. And it's a hundred times better than the straight putting. You have to dodge the ball round things like wee stone men and concrete skittles and there's a model whale where you have to putt your ball clean through its mouth and then run round the other side and catch it coming out the arse.

The mouth on this whale was about the size you would expect to find on a goldfish and you were hard at it to putt your ball through the mouth of that thing.

'Will you hurry up!' this big lad says.

'Shut your pus!'

'Make me!' he says, and shoves me on my arse. The man shouts over and tells the big lad to behave and to leave me alone or he'll be put off the golf altogether.

When I'm done with the whale the rest is easy and when I give the man his stuff back I run off to see what's next. It's a fair sized park, with its own wee farm, where you have rabbits, guinea pigs, goats and an old donkey that just stands and does bugger all. After that you've got a dose of birds in cages to look at and when I hear 'Pretty Polly' I spin round and see a parrot.

'Did you hear that?' I say to another lad.

'Aye,' he says.

'It was that bird!'

This other lad and me look at the parrot and when I tell it to say something else the matron says parrots don't take orders from anybody and just speak when they feel like it. I pretend I'm interested in some other birds and sure enough the parrot starts up again. And the words it comes out with this time has the matron raging and she moves us on and that's us finished with it.

When it's time for our picnic, the grub comes out of big laundry baskets and it's not just the Home bairns they have to feed but every other bairn that attends the Sunday school and more bairns on top of that that's maybe just thinking about starting the Sunday school. And there's a dose of sandwiches and gallons of juice to drink.

I'm eating my piece and a wee lassie's gawking at me.

'What are you looking at?'

'Shut your pus, Home boy!'

I throw my juice over the front of her dress and she goes off her head and catches me with a kick. The matron's onto me quick before I can get back at her and she's smirking when I get a slap round the lug.

When we're done with the picnic, the next thing's a ride round the whole park in carriages that are pulled by a tractor. I'm the first one on that and I tell the driver to start up his tractor and get moving and he says to wait until more bairns come to fill it. I'm out again quick and tell the matron to get all the bairns on the tractor and she tells me to get back on the thing and wait. When we finally get going you can see things you never knew were in the park and it's the pond and boats that interest me most and that's where we go next.

We're at the pond and the queue's about a mile long so when I see people getting out a boat I jump in quick.

'Hey you, wee boy, take your place in the queue,' the boatman shouts.

I pay him no heed and the matron roars. 'Get out that boat now Sandy Reid and get yourself to the back of the queue!'

The lassie I put the juice over is smirking and it's the same with the big lad that put me on my arse earlier at the golf. The matron's quick to tell me that I'll not be rowing the boat and she says she has a man from the church to do that for us. Finally it's our turn and what a carry-on the matron has getting in that boat. The church man has to take her hand and help her aboard and when the boat starts rocking I tell her to hurry up and sit on her arse and she says if I keep the language up, she'll put me ashore and that will be the end of the boat trip.

It's two oars you have with this type of boat and the church man has a job working with them, but once he has the idea he's fine and I tell him which bit of the pond to make for. After a wee while I ask if he wants me to work one of the oars for him and he's glad of that because the sweat's running off his brow.

I ask how long our shot lasts and he tells me about half an hour and the matron says she thinks ten minutes will be long enough since this is our first trip and we're just starting out with boats. When I remind her I was in the Lifeboys it makes no difference to the woman and, before you know it, we're back on dry land.

We've done all there is to do in this park now and that's the picnic over with. All the bairns pile back on the bus and we head back to Greenbanks.

When the seaside mission comes to town I've been on my best behaviour for a week and I shouldn't have bothered because I only lasted a day at the thing. My behaviour is getting wilder the longer I'm in the home and the seaside mission is a new low point for me.

I'm outside the church waiting for the mission to start and it's not just the bairns from the home, but half the bairns from the town are here as well and it's swelled further yet by even more bairns that are on their holidays. There's a few folk to run this mission, but you soon find out who's in charge when two lads step forward and shout, 'Hello boys and girls,' and that's the mission officially started.

'Hello,' we roar back.

'My name's Clarence and I'm a Cool Cat!' this lad shouts.

'I'm Humphrey – and I'm a Hot Dog!' roars the other.

We're split into two groups and I'm managed by Clarence and that makes me a Cool Cat. He tells us we're going to march to the beach and that the whole town will know how happy we are because we'll be singing at the tops of our voices. 'I want them to hear you in Methil. I want them to hear you in Pittenweem and I want them to hear you in Anstruther and I want them to hear you as far away as St Andrews!' he says. Then he teaches us a song and here's the way it went.

> Follow follow – we will follow Humphrey,
> Will we heck – we'll wring his neck,
> We will follow Clarence!

And here's the song that Humphrey teaches the Hot Dogs.

> Follow follow – we will follow Clarence,
> Will we heck – we'll wring his neck,
> We will follow Humphrey!

We march to the beach. Cool Cats on one side of the road and the Hot Dogs on the other, and we're all behind Humphrey and Clarence belting out the songs at the tops of our voices.

At the beach, one of the Hot Dogs starts to get impudent with me and says the Cool Cats are rubbish and that you're better to be a Hot Dog. I get into an argument with this Hot Dog and when I land him a punch Humphrey reports me to the Greenbanks staff who say I'm not fit for the seaside mission and take me straight back to the home.

The matron's raging when I get back and says I'm meant to be an ambassador for the home and that she can't be with me all the time and that I'm a disgrace. She takes me to her office and gets the leather strap from her drawer and gives me three whacks on each hand and that stings! 'If you act like a baby, we'll treat you like a baby!' she says and marches me straight to the nursery where the other bairns are taking their nap. She points to a cot and tells me that's where I'll sleep. Next she gets a potty and says that's where I'll do my business. 'In a potty, like a bairn!' Then she says I'll be sleeping in that cot until she sees an improvement in my behaviour. She takes me to the playroom, where I've to sit on a wooden chair and stay quiet and not make a sound until the others get back.

At teatime I have to sit with the younger bairns and it's toddlers' portions on a plastic plate that they put out for me. And it's a plastic spoon I get to scoop the stuff with. Looking back, toddlers' portions were fine – at least you were still getting fed. Some of the other bairns had it worse as deprivation of meals was a common punishment in Greenbanks. If a bairn misbehaved they could have their meals taken away. Some children could go several days without food and the only thing they got at meal times was a glass of milk. They still had to join the rest of us at the dining tables where they were made to sit with their arms folded and an empty plate was placed in front of them. The empty plate was purely symbolic and used to emphasise that they were getting bugger all to eat because of their bad behaviour.

After tea the matron takes me straight back to the nursery and tells me if I need to pee then I have to do it in the potty. Then I've to wash the potty out and let her see that it's been properly cleaned and is shining.

I ask what happens if I need a shite and that earns me a slap in the lug. She says if I need a number two then that's to go in the pot too. I don't want to do that and keep it back for days and refuse to sit on the potty. My stomach aches and when I can't hold out any longer she stands over me as I shit in the pot.

With no school, I'm in the nursery day and night and I'm only allowed up for my meals. With the bairns' portions they're feeding me I'm half starved and cramped to bits curled up in that wee cot all the time. My sister tries to help me and brings a biscuit or piece up to the nursery at night if she can. But if she's caught doing that, she'll be murdered, and she's got to be very careful.

Last thing at night I get out the cot and stand looking out the nursery window. I'm waiting for Maggie to wave to me from the girls' dormitory window across the yard. She does this before she goes to her bed every night and that makes me feel better about things. After two weeks I'm put back to regular meals and allowed back to my own bed in the dormitory. It has been a tough fortnight and not one I want to repeat.

An old woman stays next to the station and can't get about much on her two wasted legs. One day the sticks are holding her up at her front door and she shouts to me. 'Hey you – wee laddie. Run to the shop and get a message for me.'

When I'm back with the stuff she says to sit with her at the fire.

'Your house stinks of cat's pish,' I say.

'You'll get used to it,' she says.

'What do you mean I'll get used to it?'

'I'll be needing you every day for the shop, so you'll be in here a lot.'

I shift a cat and sit on a chair to look at her. 'What's that on your leg?' I ask.

'Grannies' tartan.'

'Can I catch it?'

'No,' she laughs, 'you can't catch that! That's got with sitting next to the fire all day – it burns your legs you see.'

'Why do you sit next to the fire all day if it gives you the grannies' tartan?'

'Because it's a cold house! What's your name?'

'Sandy.'

'Sandy what?'

'Sandy Reid.'

'I'm Sadie Smith – you can call me Sadie.'

'Aye, Sadie.'

'Do you like the school?'

'Not much Sadie.'

'What's your teacher's name?'

'Mrs Martin, Sadie.'

'I know her, she stays in Scoonie Road – and a nice woman she is too.'

'She's taking me to her house for my tea sometime, Sadie.'

'Is she?'

'Aye, Sadie.'

'That'll be good, you'll like that.'

'Aye, Sadie.'

'Look lad, you don't have to call me Sadie all the time.'

'Do you prefer Mrs Smith?'

'No, Sadie's fine, but you can speak to a person without having to say their name all the time Sandy.'

'Aye.'

'Do you like the home?'

'No.'

'How no?'

'I just don't.'

'Have you a mum and dad?'

'Aye.'

'Where are they?'

'I don't know.'

'Have you any brothers or sisters?'

'Just a sister.'

'A big sister, or a wee sister?'

'Big sister.'

'What's her name?'

'Maggie – Maggie Reid.'

'Is she in the home too?'

'Aye.'

She looks at the clock. 'You better be getting off to the school now or you'll be late.'

'Aye.'

'When you pass in the morning come in to see if I need anything.'

'Aye.'

'Sometimes I've a job getting to the door if my legs are bad.'

'Aye.'

'Don't bother to chap the door, just come straight in.'

'Aye.'

She hands me a threepenny bit and when I get to the school I'm later than I've ever been before. I'm fed up with the home now and I'm fed up with the school too. So, when Mrs Martin asks me why I'm late, I don't answer, and she keeps me back at playtime.

'Can I go out Mrs Martin?'

'No.'

'How no?'

'Why were you late?'

'I ran a message for a woman.'

'And that made you late?'

'Aye.'

'You don't have time to be running messages for people in the morning Sandy. School is more important – you have to be here on time.'

'But the woman can't get to the shop.'

'Why not?'

'Because her legs are buggered.'

'What woman is this Sandy?'

'Sadie – Sadie with the two sticks.'

'Sadie Smith?'

'Aye.'

'Who stays beside the station next to your home?

'Aye.'

'I know her Sandy.'

'Aye, she says she knows you too, Mrs Martin.'

'If she asks you to run a message in the morning again, then you'll have to be quicker and be in the playground before the school bell.'

'Aye.'

'Remember that!'

'Aye, can I go out now Mrs Martin?'

'I'll be keeping you in this time to teach you a lesson Sandy, but I'll tell you what you can do.'

'What?'

'You can get yourself some coloured pencils and a bit paper and draw a picture.'

I draw a picture of Sadie standing at her gate propped up with her two sticks.

'Is that Sadie?' my teacher asks.

'Aye, I'm going to give her it after the school.'

'It's very good Sandy. You should write your name on it for her.'

'Aye, I will, so she knows who drew it.'

'That's nice, she'll like that.'

'Aye.'

'With your name on it, Sadie will see what a neat writer you are Sandy.'

'Aye.' I write my name, fold it, then stick the picture in my pocket.

'When are you taking me for my tea Mrs Martin?'

'I've telephoned the matron and she says I've to write a letter asking to have you out the home.'

'Do you still want me to come to your house?'

'Of course I do Sandy.'

'When will you write the letter?'

'Soon.'

I tell her I'm going to run away soon so she'll need to be quick. She says that's a silly idea as the people in the home will worry about me and so will she. But my mind's made up because I'm just fed up with everything and so one night I bugger off.

It's dark and I'm over the wall and there's another lad at the back of me and that's him with the harelip. We have a wigwam and a blanket and it's Letham Glen I'm headed for when I see the matron's van going about. I change direction and decide to head for the beach where we put the wigwam up on the sand next to the sea wall. Once we're sorted out we start yapping.

I ask him what he's in the home for and he tells me his mother died and that his father couldn't look after him so he was put in the home. He asks about my folk and I tell him I don't know much about them but my sister does and if we're captured he can ask her about them. After a while he falls asleep and I fall asleep too.

After midnight we're wakened by two policemen and they take us back to the home. The matron's waiting for us with some of the other staff in their night clothes. The police talk to them and we're left sitting on the wooden bench outside the office.

He asks me what will happen to us and I say we'll get the belt for sure and a dose of other things and he bursts into tears. The police leave and we're called to the office. We get a long lecture about the police having to look for us, how everyone was worried, and how she and the rest of the staff could not go to bed until we were found and brought safely back to the home. She thinks it's all my fault and says that the other lad wouldn't have the intelligence to run off on his own. She thinks I planned the whole thing and when he says that I asked him to run away with me, she tells him to shut up.

She tells me I'm a very bad boy and that she'll be speaking to the Welfare about me and that if I keep up with the bad behaviour, I might even be sent to another place, far away from Maggie and then how would we see each other. We get six of the strap on each hand before we're packed off to bed.

The next morning they come for us early and we're back sitting on the bench outside the matron's office. I'm wondering what's happening now and when the police arrive I think they're going to take me to another place straight away and that this will be the end of me and Maggie. The police drive us back to the beach and this time the tide's in and the water's halfway up the sea wall. 'You could have been drowned if we never got you last night,' a policeman says, and he gives us both a few slaps round the ear. After that we're taken back to the home for breakfast then packed off to school.

Mary goes in the shop and he waits outside.

'It's a while since you've been in here Mary,' the woman says.

'Aye.'

'I was told you were in Dundee and had a house.'

'Aye, I did. But I'm finished with that and back on the road now.'

The woman looks out the window. 'I see you have Henry waiting for you.'

'Aye.'

'I heard he was in Perth prison for a while.'

'Aye.'

'So he's out now and you're back with him?'

'Aye.'

'That was a tragic thing to happen to your Davie.'

'Aye.'

'You've been through the wars Mary. Life can be cruel at times.'

'Aye.'

'Let's just hope nothing else bad happens to you Mary. You've had more than your fair share of troubles.'

'Aye.'

'Will you hurry up Mary!' Henry shouts from the street.

'Impatient bugger. What can I get you Mary?'

'A bottle of wine.'

'Is it for him?'

'Aye.'

'You're not drinking yourself, are you?'

'No, can you just give me the bottle, before he comes in this shop roaring!'

They sit across from the post office and Sandy and Peggy come along.

'See a wee taste from you Henry,' Sandy says.

'Aye, help yourself.' Henry hands him the bottle.

'Mind we're going to Leven, Sandy,' Peggy says.

'Aye, I'll no be long.'

'You know what your brother's like once he gets a taste for the peeve Mary.'

'Aye Peggy, you're better to pull him away now, or you'll never see Leven today.'

'Where have you been this last few weeks Mary? I've no seen you about.'

'We were camped over at Thornton. In with his people.'

'What a carry-on they buggers keep with the peeve. You'll be glad to be out of there Mary?'

'Aye.'

'Where's your camp, have you left it in Thornton?'

'Aye, but my brother Davie says he'll shift it and bring it down for me soon. I told him we'd be round about you and Sandy.'

'You can lie in with us for now Mary. He might be a few days yet, you know what he's like.'

'Aye.'

'Right Sandy, are you ready? We need to be getting on for Leven.'

'Hold on Peggy, there's plenty time woman. You can't just drink half a man's bottle then bugger off. I'll need to buy a bottle myself.'

'That's him started Mary.'

'Aye, he's got a taste for it now Peggy.'

'Away in the shop and get another bottle Peggy,' he says.

The two women get more wine and a police car stops beside

Sandy and Henry. 'If you're drinking, get yourselves away out the road and into a field or some wood, where you won't be bothering people.'

'Aye we'll do that Officer. Make that four bottles Peggy,' Sandy shouts.

'That's the money for his bagpipes he's away to drink now Mary.'

'Aye.'

'He leaves his pipes with a man when he needs a peeve and gets a few coppers for them. I was going to get them back for him today, but that'll be the money gone now that he's started peeving with Henry.'

They come out the shop and Peggy hands the bottles to Sandy. 'Are you no going to wait until we're out the town man?'

'No, we'll just drink them here.'

'You heard what the policeman said Sandy. You'll end up getting lifted and it will be the same for you Henry.'

'I'm no heeding what the Hornie says Peggy.'

'Well I'll no be hanging about here to get lifted along with you.'

'Please yourself.'

'Aye, I will. Come on Mary, we'll leave the two buggers to get on with it.'

When they're alone Mary says, 'There's a home in Leven I was going to try Peggy.'

'For the bairns?'

'Aye.'

'You've tried near every children's home in the County of Fife Mary. Have you not tried that one before?'

'Aye.'

'There's no sense to it Mary. Even if you do get the right place, I don't think they would tell you if the bairns were there or not.'

'This place is called Greenbanks Home.'

'Aye, I know where it is, it's next to the railway station.'

'Aye, that's right. I'm going to give it another try Peggy.'

'Are you going there now Mary?'

'Aye.'

'I'll come with you, there's no sense to me hanging about this place when they're on the peeve.'

When they get to Greenbanks Home, Peggy says she'll wait at the gate, while Mary goes to the door.

'Do you think the bairns will be here Peggy?'

'You'll not know until you ask Mary.'

'Aye, you're right, I'll away and have a look.'

'I'll be waiting here for you. Good luck Mary.'

Mary walks up the drive and rings the bell. A member of staff answers. 'Who are you and what do you want?'

'My name's Mary Reid and I was wondering if my bairns are in this home.'

'What's the names of your children?'

'Sandy and Maggie Reid.'

'Wait here, I'll get the matron.'

'Aye.'

It's a few minutes until the matron arrives.

'Who are you?' the matron says.

'Mary Reid.'

'What do you want?'

'I was wondering if you have my bairns in your home?'

'What's their names?'

'Sandy and Maggie Reid.'

'Oh, them.'

'Aye, are they here?' Mary's face lights up.

'They were here, but not any more. They left a couple of days ago.'

'Left – what do you mean left?'

'The Welfare found a new foster family for them and they've been boarded out.'

'Boarded out? Where have they gone? Where do the new foster people live?'

'That's something you'll have to see the Welfare about. I can't give out that type of information Mrs Reid. You'll have to talk to the Welfare.'

'But you're the matron. You must know where they've gone.'

'Look, even if I do know, I can't tell you where they are Mrs Reid. If you want any information about your children, you have to go to the Welfare!'

'I'm forever at the Welfare. Sometimes I've sat the whole day in the County Buildings and they never tell me anything. If you know where they are, why can't you tell me?'

'I can't tell you anything Mrs Reid. Now I'm a busy woman with children to look after – you'll need to go!'

'What are they like?'

'Who?'

'Sandy and Maggie.'

'Well, I suppose they're just like any other children.'

'What do they look like? Are they doing well at the school? Maggie will be getting a big lassie now. What's Sandy like?'

'Look, Mrs Reid, I'm a busy woman. I really have to go now!'

'Have you any photographs of them? Could you give me one? The home must take photos of the bairns – you must have one?'

'You have to go to the Welfare Mrs Reid.'

'Fuck the Welfare! You know my bairns – tell me what they're like!'

'Mrs Reid, your children have a new foster family now. A family that will care for them and give them all that they need.'

'Aye, but I'm their mother.'

'I know you're their mother Mrs Reid. But if the children were to see you, don't you think that would upset them?'

'How would my bairns be upset about seeing their own mother?'

'It would make them anxious. They might not do so well at the school and maybe it would set them back if they were to see you.'

'That's rubbish!'

'Is it?'

'Aye, my bairns would be glad to see me. Maggie would still remember me.'

'But Sandy has never seen you. Can you imagine what a shock it would be for him to see his mother for the first time?'

'I think he would be fine with it.'

'Give the bairns a chance Mrs Reid – let them go.'

'I'll never let my bairns go. I'll never stop trying to get them back!'

The door closes and Mary goes back to Peggy.

'Well?'

'They're not in there Peggy.'

'That's a shame Mary.'

'But they were there and they shifted them a few days ago.'

'Did they?'

'Aye, and if I'd been a few days earlier, I would have seen them Peggy.'

'Did they tell you where they shifted them to?'

'They just said it was a new foster family they had for them.' Mary leaned back against the wall.

'Are you alright Mary? You look a bit no well.' Peggy was concerned.

'I'm fine.'

'It's the shock to you. Sit down on the pavement for a minute.'

'No, I'm fine Peggy. Let's just get away from this place.'

As they walk, Mary begins to feel more unwell. 'You're not looking good Mary. Are you sure you're alright?'

'Aye, I'm fine Peggy, just a bit worn out.'

'I'll knock a door and see if I can get a drop water for you.'

Mary leans on the gate as Peggy chaps the door. 'I don't think there's anyone in here Mary, I'll try another door.'

'What do you want?' a woman shouts. 'I need time to answer the door. I'm no very fast on my sticks.'

'Have you some water for my friend here Mrs? She's taken no well.'

The woman looks down the path at Mary. 'She looks a bit funny, bring her into the house.'

'Are you sure?'

'Aye, bring her in.'

The woman shifts cats to let Mary sit.

'Away to the kitchen and get some water for your friend.'

Peggy brings water and shifts more cats to get herself a seat next to Mary.

'Are you tinks?'

'Here, drink this Mary.'

'Thanks Peggy, I was sore needing that. I was starting to feel dizzy.'

'Are you two tinks?'

'You'll feel better now.'

'I can smell the wood reek off you. You must be tinks. Where are you camped?'

'Upper Largo,' Peggy says.

'You've a bit to walk out there, have you no?'

'Aye.'

'What's your name?'

'Peggy.'

'And what's her name?'

'Mary.'

'I'm Sadie Smith – you can call me Sadie.'

'Mary's my sister-in-law. She took no well in the street.'

'Are you feeling a bit better now Mary?' Sadie asks.

'Aye, it's good of you to let us in.'

'That's alright, if I'm ever out your way I'll stop in at your tent sometime.'

'And you'd be welcome,' Peggy says. 'It's no very often we're invited into people's houses.'

'Would you like a cup of tea?'

'Aye, that would be good,' Peggy says.

'What about you Mary, do you want some tea? It'll make you feel better.'

'Aye, that would be braw Sadie.'

'Would you make it for me Peggy? I'm not very good on my feet.'

'Aye, just you sit on your arse Sadie. I'll make it no bother.'

'So you're feeling better now Mary. What came over you lass?'

'Och, I just felt a bit funny, that's all.'

'A good cup of tea will make you feel a lot better.'

'Aye.'

'It must be hard for you in the winter in they tents that you have. All that frost and the freezing wind must get to you. This old house rattles and shakes and I can even have ice on the window sills in the morning when it's bad. It must be much worse in your wee tents.'

'We're fine in the tents Sadie. We have a fire going and we're likely warmer than you would be in this wee house.'

'I could believe that. I'm forever packing the coal onto that fire in the winter. I'm hard pushed to keep it going! If it wasn't for the man next door I would freeze. He brings the coal in for me, I could never manage to lift the coal bucket myself.'

'That's good of him.'

'Aye, I'm lucky to have him next door. You get people that would do nothing for you.'

'Aye, you're right Sadie.'

'Well, I suppose you would know more about that than me Mary.'

'Aye.'

'Have you any milk Sadie?' Peggy shouts from the kitchen.

'Damn! I forgot about milk. The wee lad that runs to the shop for me hasn't been in this last few days. I wonder where he is, the wee rascal. He usually comes in every morning to see if I need anything.'

'That's bairns for you Sadie,' Peggy says. 'Here one minute and gone the next.' Mary gives her a look. 'Sorry Mary. I wasn't thinking when I said that.'

'I can take my tea without milk,' Sadie says.

'I often drink the stuff with nothing in it – just the bare leaves,' Peggy says.

'I'm the same,' Mary says.

'So what brings you into Leven?'

'Mary was hoping to see her bairns,' Peggy says.

'See her bairns?'

'Aye, the Welfare's got them and we thought they might be in the home here.'

'Greenbanks, the home up the road?'

'Aye.'

'She's been round every home in the county and she's never found her bairns yet. They were in that Greenbanks Home right enough, but the matron told her they've been boarded out.'

'I see different faces from that place all the time. Poor wee souls. What's the names of your bairns Mary?'

'Sandy and Maggie Reid.'

'Sandy!'

'Aye.'

'Wee Sandy Reid!'

'Aye!' Mary's face lights up. 'Do you know him – have you seen him Sadie?'

'Seen him! I would see him just about every day – that's the wee laddie I was just talking about. The one that gets the shop for me!'

'Oh Sadie, what's he like?'

'He's a braw wee bairn Mary – a lovely wee boy!'

'Are you alright Mary?' Peggy asks.

'Aye, I'm fine Peggy.'

'It's a bit of a shock to her Sadie. She's never seen her bairns since the day they were taken away from her.'

'When did the Welfare take your bairns Mary?'

'Sandy was just a baby at the time,' Peggy says.

'Oh Mary – I feel so sorry for you. Sandy's a braw wee bairn.'

'Did you ever see Maggie?' Mary asks.

'I wouldn't know her. Like I was just saying, there were always different bairns coming and going from that place. I couldn't put names to them all Mary. It would just be Sandy that I knew. That was the wee lad that got the shop for me.'

'She doesn't even have a photo of her bairns,' Peggy says.

'That's sad. Not even one photo of your own wee bairns. You must be tormented Mary.'

'Aye, I think about them every day Sadie.'

'Hold on,' Sadie says. 'Hold on just one minute till I get up.'

She shuffles over to the sideboard and opens a drawer. 'I've something here that I want to show you.' She goes back to Mary and hands her a folded piece of paper.

'What's this?' Mary asks.

'Open it and have a look.'

'Oh, it's a wee picture of you with your two sticks Sadie. What a braw wee picture, did your grandson draw that for you?'

'No, look at the name on it Mary.'

'Sandy?'

'That's right. It was your wee laddie that drew that picture. Your own bairn – Sandy!'

'Wipe your eyes Mary.' Sadie gives her a hanky. 'You don't want to be putting tears all over your bairn's picture now, do you?'

'Thank you . . . Thank you for showing me your picture Sadie.'

'It's not my picture.' Sadie's hand was on Mary's. 'It's your picture now Mary.'

'How long will we be in this place Maggie?'

'I don't know Sandy.'

'How long do you think we'll be here?'

'I don't know.'

'Do you think they like us?'

'I don't know!'

'What do you think?'

'I don't know!'

'Do you think this place will be better than the home?'

'Aye, probably, I was getting sick of Greenbanks.'

'Do you think they'll put us to school here Maggie?'

'Aye.'

'What school?'

'I don't know. How should I know what school they'll put us to?'

'Do you like the man Maggie?'

'I don't know him.'

'Do you like the woman?'

'Will you shut up!'

'I'm only asking, do you like her?'

'I don't know. Ask me in the morning.'

'In the morning?'

'Aye, now go to sleep Sandy.'

'This room's wee.'

'Aye, wee and better.'

'How?'

'How what?'

'How's it better?'

'Because it's fucking smaller – now shut up!'

'Maggie?'

'What!'

'I'm glad we're sharing a room.'

'How?'

'Because we can talk.'

'We're not talking all night Sandy!'

'It's not like the home where we were in different dormitories.'

'No.'

'What do you think they'll give us for breakfast Maggie?'

'I don't know.'

'Remember the last foster home where that man cooked the grub and it was rubbish.'

'Aye.'

'I think it will be her that cooks in this place – what do you think?'

'Aye, she'll cook.'

'So what do you think we'll get for breakfast?'

'I don't know.'

'But what do you think we'll get?'

'How the hell should I know what we'll get. Now shut up and go to sleep!'

'Maggie?'

'What!'

'Where are we?'

'I don't know.'

'Will you find out Maggie?'

'Aye, I'll find out in the morning.'

'Goodnight Maggie.'

'Goodnight Sandy.'

* * *

We're in the park with a dose of other bairns. Some girl asks Maggie where we're from and Maggie says Leven. The lassie says she has an uncle in Leven and when she visits him they go down to the beach and let his dog run about. I tell her we were in a home in Leven and I slept on the beach when I ran away from the place and Maggie tells me to shut up. But this lassie has a big nose and asks why we were in the home and that gets Maggie raging.

'It's none of your business!' she says.

'I was only asking,' says the lassie.

'My mum says you'll be bad bairns if you're from a home,' this other lad says.

'Well you better not play with us then!' Maggie shouts.

They walk away and Maggie says that's us ruined because I opened my big mouth about the home. We'll never have any pals in this place now because people don't want to play with you if you've come from a home.

I say we can try some other bairns over at the swings, but she says I'm daft and that nobody will want to know us now and that it's all my fault. I tell her to shut her pus and she smacks me one.

The woman says to call her Auntie Flo and to call him Uncle Bert. It's a good wee house they have in Glenrothes and the bit where we are is called Woodside. We've to share a room to start with until they get my room ready. I've to share a bed with Maggie, until the Welfare can come up with another bed for me.

This is a big change from Greenbanks and you've to get used to being in a house again. In Greenbanks you had bairns running about and roaring at the tops of their voices and this woman says you don't have to do that here. 'We can hear you just fine without you having to shout,' she says.

It's so quiet in this place you can hear the clock on the

mantelpiece ticking. The woman wants you to keep quiet all the time because the noise bothers her and she's forever at the doctor to see if he can fix her nerves.

It's an open fire they have, but they never burn sticks and it's just coal they heap on it. A wire guard goes all the way round the fire and you can't get near the thing for a heat. 'Keep back, or you'll be burnt,' she says. On top of the guard she has trousers, jumpers, socks and a dose of woman's stuff that she's trying to get dry. He says the stuff should be drying outside and she tells him people don't want to see your dirty washing flying in the wind and he says once it's washed it's clean.

They sit in chairs next to the fire, him in one chair and her in the other and we play on the floor further back. 'If anything spits from that fire it won't get you,' she says. We've to play quiet and if you make a noise that's her nerves shattered and she packs you off to bed with no supper.

On Saturdays she goes shopping and we're left with him. His pals come in to watch the telly and it's the wrestling they like. When that's finished me and her have a wrestling match and Uncle Bert has a sixpence for the winner. Some of the lads cheer for me and some of the lads cheer for her and we get stuck right into each other for that sixpence. They move the fireguard to make room for the fight and one time her head lands in the fire after a good push from me. The hair goes whoosh and she packs in with fright so that's the wrestling match finished and the sixpence is mine.

That man has a thing like a tea stain on his face and when I ask what it is he tells me it's a birthmark. He's a lazy bugger this man and never bothers to go out the front door and we're sent for anything that he needs from the shop. One afternoon he wants a fill for his pipe and hands Maggie a ten shilling note. On the way to the shop we pass the park where a dose of bairns are playing.

'C'mon we'll go over and see them,' Maggie says.

The lassie that asked us about the home is there and Maggie has the ten shilling note out her pocket and in her hands now.

'What's that you have there?' says the lassie.

'It's my pocket money,' Maggie says.

'Let me see, how much do you have?'

'Ten bob,' Maggie says, holding it up for all to see.

'And that's your pocket money?'

'Aye.'

'I only get a shilling, how come you get all that?'

'Because the foster folk like us and they told me I can expect ten shillings every week for my pocket money.'

She looks at me. 'How much do you get?'

Maggie answers for me. 'A half crown.'

'A half crown my arse. Show me your half crown!'

'He spent it this morning,' Maggie says.

'I don't believe you. I bet you've been sent to the shop and that money's for a message!'

'You can watch me spend it if you like,' says Maggie, and I give her a look.

'Right, I will! C'mon everybody, we'll go to the shop with her and see if she spends the ten shillings!'

We walk to the shop with a dose of bairns round us and I ask Maggie what she's going to do now, but she pays me no heed.

At the shop Maggie picks a few things out for herself and the lassie says to get her something as well. Before you know it all the bairns have their fingers in the penny and halfpenny trays and the man asks Maggie if she has the money to pay for it all. She shows him the ten shilling note and he's fine with that and everyone gets to pick sweets out the trays. I'm the last to take a handful and when Maggie hands the note over, the man says she can add to that note or put some of the sweets back. She puts her own sweets back and the man says he needs more back yet. She looks at me and I look at the man who has his hand out waiting. I hand my sweets back to him and he's fine with that and me and her leave the shop with bugger all.

In the park I'm cracking with the lads and she's cracking with the lassies and they're all munching their sweets and that's us accepted now. Some bairns wander off and others get called for their tea and it's only me and her left in the park.

'What are you going to tell the man, Maggie?'

'I'll just say I lost the ten shillings.'

'Do you think he'll believe you?'

'Aye, he's fine with us, you can work that man.'

'What about her?' I say.

'It's no her money, the ten shillings belonged him.'

'Aye, but she'll want to know what happened to it.'

'Will you stop worrying, she'll no be back yet anyway.'

At the house I let her go in first. 'You took your time at the shop – where's my baccy?' he says.

She's there too, sitting in her chair, with the knitting pins under her arms and looking over her glasses at us.

'Aye well . . .' says Maggie.

'Well what?' he says.

'I lost the money.'

'You lost it?'

'Aye.'

'The whole ten bob?'

'Aye.'

'Where did you lose it?' she says.

'I dropped it,' Maggie says.

'You're a liar!'

'No, it's true, I lost it.'

'You stole it!' she says.

'I never.'

'Don't lie – admit you stole the money!'

'I never.'

'Why did you trust her with ten shillings Bert?'

'She's been to the shop before for me.'

'She's a thief! You should know better than to trust her with a ten shilling note you fool. That lassie would pinch the matter out your eye!'

'I don't think she stole it Flo. Maybe she did lose it.'

She's over to Maggie and gets a grip of her hair. 'Admit you stole it, you thief!'

'I never stole it, I lost it. I'll go out and see if I can find it.'

'You won't find it because you've spent it!' She gives her a slap, then another and another yet. 'Away up the stair with you and get out my sight!'

Maggie's away and I'm left with them.

'Did your sister spend the ten shillings?' she says.

'She lost it.'

'Another liar.' She gives me a slap too.

'There's no sense in hitting him Flo. If it's spent then it was her that spent it.'

'You get up the stairs too,' she says.

I'm in the room with Maggie and she says, 'I'll tell her I spent it.'

'What for?'

'Because that'll be it over with.'

'She'll be raging Maggie.'

'Aye, but I'll say it was me that spent it and no you.'

'I'm no caring what she thinks Maggie.'

'You just keep your mouth shut Sandy and leave it to me.'

When she comes to the room she has a schoolteacher's strap in her hand and it's six whacks each we get. She says she'll have the Welfare onto us and if she hears one more cheep out of us tonight we'll get the same again.

Two days later the Welfare woman comes and she sits at the table next to the window and has tea and biscuits with Auntie Flo. We listen as she tells her all about our bad behaviour, that we stole money, that we're both liars and 'sleekit' and not to be trusted. She doesn't think she's managing to cope with us. She says we swear like troopers and that she's not used to hearing that kind of stuff from the mouths of bairns and maybe we'll have to go back to the home to save her nerves. The Welfare woman says she'll take us out in the car and have a good talk with us.

When she has us away from the place she tells us that this is our very last chance with a foster family and that we have to make it work. If you mess up here, then there's nothing left for you and it'll be the home for us until we're grown up. We've to apologise to Aunt Flo and promise to behave and promise not to tell any more lies and promise that there will be no more stealing. I'm checked about my swearing and she says if she hears any more about bad language coming from my mouth then I'll be for the high jump. We've to think about the woman's nerves and try to be good bairns then Auntie Flo will be fine with us and this place will work out.

At the new school, Maggie's getting bullied and one day a dose of bairns chase her right to the door of the foster home and Auntie Flo's raging. 'I'll be down to that school to see the headmaster about you lot,' she shouts to them.

She keeps her word and the next day she's at the school. The lassies are called to the headmaster's office and Maggie has to tell him what happened. She never liked to say anything about it in front of the other bairns and the headmaster thinks she's just making up stories. If she's getting a hiding then it's probably because she torments the life out the other bairns he says.

We're still sharing a bed and I'm getting sick of her pishing it every night. The woman has Maggie to the doctor and he hands over a dose of pills that's supposed to stop you pishing the bed but they don't work for Maggie.

'I'm not going to school,' she says to me one day.

'How no?'

'Because I don't like it.'

'What are you going to do?'

'I'll just bugger about until it's time up.'

'Where about?'

'In the woods.'

'I'll come with you.'

'Come if you want.'

We wander through the streets and reach the edge of town. I'm wearing short trousers and she has a skirt and socks. We go down a wee road and climb over a gate and that's us in a cow field. The cows never bother with us and she's striding in front and I'm straggling behind her.

'Slow down Maggie,' I shout.

'Hurry up,' she says.

'Maggie!'

'What?'

'I've stood in shite.'

'You should look where you're putting your feet Sandy.'

'It's all over my shoe and halfway up my sock!'

'Wipe your shoe on the grass.'

I sit down and she's over to me and so are the cows. They sniff and look at us and when I get up again they move out the way. After the cow field it's a wood we're in and I follow her along a path.

'Do you know this wood Maggie?'

'No.'

'Have you never been in it before?'

'No.'

'Do you know where you're going?'

'Aye.'

'How do you know where you're going?'

'I just do.'

'Maybe we'll get lost.'

'Don't be daft.'

'We might if you don't know the place.'

'One wood's the same as any other wood Sandy. You can't get lost in a wood!'

'What will they say about us no being at the school Maggie?'

'I don't know.'

'What do you think they'll say?'

'I don't care.'

'Maybe we'll get put back to the home for this Maggie.'

'Aye, maybe.'

'Are you no bothered Maggie?'

'No.'

'What happens if they put you back and I'm left with the foster folk?'

'They'll no do that Sandy.'

'How do you know?'

'I just do.'

'Are you sure Maggie?'

'Aye.'

'Och, I'm no bothered either then.'

We come to a clear bit next to a burn and she pulls matches from her pocket.

'Where did you get the matches Maggie?'

'From his pocket. Now away and get sticks and we'll get a wee fire going.'

We snap branches and put them in a pile and Maggie puts a match to them. She gets a good blaze going and we sit. She just looks at the fire and it's a while before she says anything.

'Take off your sock and give it a wash in the burn.'

'It'll get wet.'

'I'll dry it for you.'

I dip the sock in the burn and when I'm back she hangs it on a stick next to the fire to dry.

'What a reek Maggie.'

'Sit this side, that way you'll no get smoke in your eyes.'

I sit beside her. 'This is braw Maggie.'

'Aye.'

'Better than the school.'

'Aye.'

'Will we be here when it gets dark?'

'No.'

'How no?'

'Because we'll need to be back in time for the school coming out.'

'How will you know when it's time for the school to come out Maggie?'

'Don't worry about that Sandy. I'll know,' she says.

'But how will you know Maggie?'

'I just will.'

'Tell me how?'

'Shut up!'

We put more sticks on the fire. Maggie says she doesn't like the people we're staying with and I say I don't either. You can live in a wood like this forever she says. All you need is a wee fire and you can get all the grub you can eat from farms. They give you any kind of thing you want at a farm. You can have bread, milk, eggs, even a bit cheese if you like, you just have to ask and the country people give it to you. She tells me that's what our mammy did all the time. She would go to any farm and just ask for anything she wanted and the country folk would give it to her no bother.

'I need to go Maggie.'

'Go behind a bush.'

'It's a shite I'm needing!'

'Go behind a bush!'

'What will I wipe my arse with?'

'Gather a bit moss, or leaves will do you fine.'

'I'm no doing that.'

'How no?'

'Because I'm no!'

'Well, use your underpants then.'

'My underpants?'

'Aye.'

'I'm no using them!'

'How no?'

'Because I'll no be able to wear them after that.'

'Throw them away you fool!'

'Aye, ok.'

When I'm back she says nothing and sits looking at the fire and if I say anything she tells me to shut up. She gets moods like this, where her mind's somewhere else, someplace far away and I just sit quiet.

After a while she wants to move and stamps the fire out with her foot. We cross a stone bridge and she tells me there's fish in the burn and if I look closely I'll see them. I look and there's a few brown trout going about. We go up the side of a field, then through a gate and into another field. She walks and walks and I follow.

We come to a farm and a wee collie dog comes running to meet us and Maggie claps it. That's a good enough wee dog she says and I clap it too. We go to the farmhouse and the wee dog follows wagging its tail. Maggie chaps the door and it's a fat woman with big arms and a red face that answers.

'Can you give us a piece Mrs?' Maggie says.

'What do you want a piece for?'

'Because we're hungry.'

'Wait there,' she says, and shuts the door.

'I told you you can ask for whatever you like at a farm Sandy.'

'Aye.'

'That woman's away to get pieces for us right now.'

'Aye.'

'She'll no be long.'

'What do you think she'll put on them Maggie?'

'How should I know what she'll put on them?'

'What do you think she'll put on them?'

'You'll just have to wait and see.'

I look at the collie dog and it's still wagging its tail and still looking to be friendly with us. Before long the woman comes back and hands us the pieces and there's butter and jam on them.

'Thank you Mrs,' Maggie says.

'You're welcome,' she says.

'We were sore needing this.'

When we're finished the woman asks where we're from and Maggie says Glenrothes.

'Where about in Glenrothes?' she asks.

'Woodside,' Maggie says.

'How come you're not in school today?'

'We have the day off.'

'You have the day off?'

'Aye, the school's out today.'

'What do you mean the school's out? Are all the bairns off?'

'Aye, the whole school's off. There's no bairns at the school today.'

'Except mine!' the woman says.

'Aye, well it's maybe just some of the bairns that's off. I think they only cancelled half the school.'

'You're meant to be in the school,' she says.

'No, it's just our class that's off, our teacher took no well.'

'And you were sent home?'

'Aye.'

'Well what are you doing away out here?'

'We're out for a walk.'

'I think you need to be getting yourselves home,' she says.

We walk away and she tells us to carry straight on through the farm and keep on the dirt track until we come to the main road and that will take us right back to Glenrothes.

We go and the wee collie dog follows and she never bothers to shout it back to her. We keep on the track until we get to the road and that's where the wee dog stops. Maggie tries to coax it to follow us but it won't budge and just sits on its arse. 'That's as far as that wee dog's allowed to go,' Maggie says, and we leave it sitting at the road end.

We walk for a bit and a tractor stops. 'Get in the bogey you two,' the man shouts to us. We get in and he takes us to Glenrothes. When he's gone we walk the short distance to Woodside and sit in the park. When the bairns start coming out the school Maggie says that it's time for us to go back to the house.

We can see the foster woman looking out the window and I say, 'Do you think she knows we've no been in school today Maggie?'

'Aye, maybe she does.'

'What will we say?'

'I'll just say I was sick.'

'What about me Maggie, what will I say?'

'Say you were sick too.'

'Do you think she'll believe us?'

'Aye.'

The woman never believed a word we said and took the belt to us and said she'd be getting the Welfare woman back to the house to see about the carry-on we've been keeping. Maggie gets the blame for me being off the school but she never bothers to make excuses and the woman goes off her head shouting at her. She puts us straight to bed to give her some peace and I ask Maggie if she thinks we'll be put back to the home for this. She says she doesn't care if we are and that she would be glad to leave this place anyway because we would be better off in the home where we have more pals and the bairns are more like us.

Miss Black the Welfare woman comes and Auntie Flo bleats on about all the bad things we've done to upset her. Miss Black says that Auntie Flo was right to take a firm hand with us and that if she hadn't done that then we would just run right over her and take advantage of her good nature and softness and things would only get worse. 'Bairns need to know their place,' she says.

'I think Mary should have stayed with us a bit longer Sandy.'

'Aye.'

'The woman was worn out.'

'Aye.'

'Near every bone in her face was broken. Did you see that Sandy?'

'Aye.'

'The rain was coming down in buckets last night when she left.'

'Aye.'

'She'll be soaked to the bones by the time she lands in Dundee.'

'Aye.'

'She never had much to say, did she?'

'No.'

'I think her mind's away now. All she thinks about is the bairns and that's why she has nothing much to say.'

'Aye.'

'She could hardly get a breath. Did you notice that too Sandy?'

'I could see that Peggy.'

'It's the lying out that does that to her.'

'Aye.'

'He'll no bother to put a camp up when he's peeving like that.'

'No.'

'He'll just sit where he is and no bother if it rains or snows.'

'If they had the bairns he would put a camp up Peggy.'

'Do you think so?'

'Aye.'

'I don't think he would bother his arse. Every penny that man gets he puts down his throat along with the coppers she begs at the doors. She never had much to say at all. I think she was worn out Sandy.'

'Aye, weary.'

'You should have told her to stay with us for a while.'

'You can't tell the woman what to do Peggy.'

'Aye, but she's no fit for walking Sandy.'

'She'll be fine Peggy. Stop worrying about her.'

'I think it's a doctor she's needing to fix her.'

'She'll be fine woman.'

'Do you think so?'

'Aye.'

'He'll be looking for her when he's sober.'

'Aye.'

'And he'll come looking here.'

'Aye.'

'She said no to say anything about her going back to Dundee.'

'I don't know why she bothers with Dundee Peggy. It's no like she has the house any more. What's she going to do over there?'

'She'll likely go to see the mission folk.'

'Aye, they'll sort her out right enough and give her somewhere to lie down.'

'It pished with rain the night she left.'

'Aye.'

'It poured the whole night and her walking in the pishing rain and no able to catch her breath.'

'Aye.'

'When the damp gets in your bones you've to watch out Sandy. Because that could be the end of a person when the damp gets in their bones. Old Angus Macgregor was gotten dead behind a dyke. And they had that man boxed before any bugger knew he'd even died!'

'She'll be fine Peggy. She'll lie in a wood or find an old shed and keep herself out the rain.'

'I don't think she cares what happens to her Sandy. She should have stayed here with us for a while longer – she would be fine that way. I asked her to stay, but she wouldn't listen to me, she just wanted to get back to Dundee and away from him.'

'Aye.'

'You're her own brother Sandy. You should have done more for her.'

'What was I supposed to do woman? There's nothing you can do if a person will no listen to what you're saying. She'll be fine, she can look out for herself, so stop worrying about the woman.'

'I think she should have waited and got her laddie Henry to shift her over to Dundee.'

'She'll be fine. Now will you stop worrying about her Peggy.'

It took two days for Mary to walk the distance to Dundee. The first night she never got far with the teeming rain and got herself into a thick wood with a wee fire. The next day was fair and she started to walk early but her pace was slow. A man stopped in a butcher's van and he took her a few miles along the road. He was a good enough man who had known her for years. He would give whatever he could spare when she had the bairns with her and he asked about them now. She said they were all with the Welfare and he never asked any more about them after that.

In Dundee she met with other tinkers and they asked about Henry. 'I've left him in Fife,' she said. There was drink going about and she went on her way. She walked the streets of Dundee until she was weary. She never bothered with the mission house and went to a cafe where the woman knew her and gave her soup. In the early evening it started to snow and she made her way back to her old house.

The door at 72 King Street wouldn't take the key that she had in her pocket and she knew that the locks had been changed. She threw the key in long grass and went round to the back of the house where she managed to pull one of the wooden boards off a window. She broke the glass with a stone and got herself inside.

You would think a bomb had gone off in the place. The settee was ripped to pieces and all the stuffing had been pulled from it and was lying on the floor. She could see that people had dossed there and empty wine bottles littered the floor. She went to the kitchen and all the crockery was in bits. Every single cup and plate had been smashed. Someone had used the kitchen as a shite house and even the walls were smeared. Everything was in bits. The curtains were in shreds, all the plates were smashed, the windows were cracked and the house was like a midden. The kitchen floor was covered in broken crockery and there was bugger all left in the place that had any value or could be fixed. She sat in the old armchair. The walk from Fife had taken its toll and she needed to rest. She was weary, sore and tired. The plates are broken, the piano's broken, her face is broken and her heart's broken. She gave a deep sigh and fell asleep.

18th December 1964, the week before Christmas, and there's a hard frost on the ground.

An icy wind cuts and two men stand with their hands thrust deep in their pockets.

Another pulls his collar tight about his neck. 'It's bitter,' he says.

'I don't think anyone's coming,' says another.

'Who was she?'

'Mary Reid. A tinker woman.'

'Sometimes you get a good turn out for the tinker folk. Other times you get nobody.'

He looks to the cemetery gates. 'It looks like there's no bugger coming to see this one off. I'll say a few words then we'll get to work.'

The doctor says Auntie Flo needs complete rest and that she'll get no peace with bairns running about the place so we're put back to the home. Maggie and I were just too much of a handful for them, I suppose, so we just have to get on with it. Foster homes have been difficult to find for us and I know that it's the children's homes for us, maybe for good now. I'm not bothered one way or the other as long as me and Maggie are together. We'd both like to see our mum and dad though, and the rest of our family. We never really speak about it but it's hard knowing we have people out there in the world outside and not really knowing if they're coming for us one day or not. Apart from Maggie seeing them at the school that day, there's been no more contact. We don't speak about it, but Maggie and me both know that we want to see them and to live with them again. They may have a hard way of life but surely nothing could be worse for us than this.

When we get back to Greenbanks, there's a dose of new faces but most of the bairns I know from before. There's some new staff going about, but I don't bother with them and they don't bother with me. I'm back to Parkhill School and the matron remembers to pack me off early before the other bairns. I stop at Sadie's on the way and she's pleased to see me.

'Sandy!'

'Aye.'

'I never thought I would see you again laddie. I heard you were in a new place.'

'Aye.'

'How come you're back here?'

'The foster woman took no well.'

'Oh, that's a shame. What was wrong with her?'

'Her nerves were broken with the carry-on me and my sister kept.'

I get money for the shop and when I'm back she tells me to sit with her for a wee while. She asks about my sister and I tell her she's back in the home too. She says I should bring Maggie to see her sometime. Sadie's just the same. She still has the same cheery smile, the same clothes, and I can still smell the cat's pish.

I'm fifteen minutes late for school so Mrs Martin keeps me in at playtime.

'Did you stop at Sadie's?' she asks.

'Aye.'

'Was she pleased to see you?'

'Aye.'

'Remember what I told you about getting to school on time.'

'Aye.'

'It's your first day back and you're late.'

'Aye.'

'You'll be glad to see all your pals again.'

'Aye.'

'And the matron will be pleased to have you back in the home.'

'She's no said a word to me yet.'

'She's probably been very busy Sandy.'

'Aye.'

She gives me pencils and I sit and draw pictures until the break's over.

One day I'm outside playing with the rest of the bairns when a wee lassie comes rushing out.

'Come and see this!' she roars.

We stop what we're doing and go into the playroom. You could hear a pin drop as all the bairns stand staring at the new boy. The staff say nothing and we say nothing until I break the silence.

'Look at him Maggie.'

'It's a darkie,' she says.

Nobody says a word and you would think all the bairns had been struck dumb. I decide to take a closer look at this lad.

'Don't you be going too close to that darkie,' my sister says. I pay her no heed and go up to the lad. He doesn't flinch when I get to him and stands still like a statue. I have a look at him from the back before I face him.

'What's your name?'

He doesn't answer me.

'Can you speak?'

'Yes he can speak,' the matron says.

'Tell him to say something.'

'He'll speak when he's ready to speak,' she says.

I see a tear running down the lad's cheek.

'What are you crying for?'

A few of the other bairns get closer to have a better look at him and the lad bursts into tears. The matron sends us all out to play and says to leave the lad alone until he finds his feet. We don't see much of him after that as the matron kept him back from the rest of us. After two days he's shipped out the place and that's the last we see of him.

* * *

The matron would listen at the door and if she heard any talking at night in the dormitory she was right in to catch the culprit. If nobody owned up she would just pick out bairns for punishment and it was the stone floor in the corridor you'd to stand on in your bare feet. There's a dose of rules to break in this place and one day I'm back in her office. I think she's fed up with me and she's raging this time. She starts to roar at me and I roar back and get a good dose of the belt for my cheek. When she's finished with me I'm sent to the playroom and she's right there at the back of me. All the bairns are watching and she tells me to sit on a wooden chair but I pay her no heed. She starts to roar again and Maggie's over to stand with me and gets a slap for it. That gets me wild and I pick up a chair and throw it through the window.

The matron gets the Welfare in to see me and I tell them I don't like the place. My sister says she doesn't like the place either, but Miss Black the Welfare woman just tells us to behave and Maggie's told to stay out of things that don't concern her. Miss Black seems to think that Maggie should not be concerned about me. If Maggie never got me agitated in the first place then I wouldn't be breaking windows she says. Maggie tells her she got a few slaps from the matron and Miss Black says she deserved them because it was none of her business, and she should know better than to be poking her nose in when the matron's sorting me out. She warns me not to throw any more chairs through windows then she's finished with us.

One day I never bothered going to school and wandered out to the countryside. I'm sitting with my back to a stone dyke and notice haystacks in a field. Next minute I'm over the dyke and climb to the top of one to look about the place. I jump down and climb the next one, then the next. When I'm bored with the haystacks I decide to put a match to them all, and I'm still standing there when the fire engine comes, and the police take me back to the home.

The matron says she can't do anything with me so the policeman says maybe he'd be better to have a word with me, and I'm left in the office with him. He tells me you're not supposed to burn haystacks and that it can be dangerous to do that. He says if I keep up the bad behaviour then the Welfare might have to start thinking about putting me somewhere else. He says if that happens then I might have to be separated from my sister.

When he's finished with me the matron tells me to sit on the bench outside the office until the other bairns come back from the school. I sit looking at the clock on the wall and watch the big hand clunking from minute to minute. When you're only seven years old and you've to sit on a wooden bench and not move for over three hours then the afternoon can be a long time in passing. I thought about what the policeman had said to me. I could remember my foster father at Balcarres saying the same thing. He often threatened to separate Maggie and me, but he never did. Maggie was the only person I had in the world. She was my sister – all that I had. There could be no worse punishment than to take her away from me. The Welfare would never do that. They would never separate us. Would they?

When Miss Black visits us again she asks if we like the home and Maggie tells her the place is rubbish and I say the same. Maggie asks if we'll be getting new foster parents, or will we be staying in Greenbanks forever. Miss Black says she doesn't know what will happen to us and that we'll just have to wait and see. She doesn't stay long but tells us she'll be back to visit again soon. When she leaves, Maggie says the woman never answers any of our questions or listens to a word we say.

One night I'm coming out of the toilet and Maggie pushes me back in and locks the door. She has her coat on and my coat's in her hand.

'Put this on,' she says.

'What for?'

'Just put it on and shut your pus.'

She opens the window and climbs out and I'm at the back of her. The two of us are over the wall and away through the streets. We get a country road and when a car comes she has me lying down until it passes. She never says much and just walks and walks and I follow at the back of her. After a while I get fed up walking and start to wish I'd never left the home.

'Can we stop Maggie?'

'No.'

'Why no?'

'Because.'

'Because what?'

'Because we can't.'

'I'm tired.'

'Keep walking.'

'Where are we going?'

'Shut up!'

'You shut up!'

I decide I'm not going any further and that gets Maggie raging and she takes a grip of me. 'You'll fucking walk!' she says, and slaps my lug. After a while she cuts off the road and we go up a dirt track. We see a long shed and it's packed with straw. Maggie goes in and climbs to the top of the bales and I do the same.

We're fine and warm up here and she says it will do for the night.

She says she heard the matron saying that I would be shifted out the place soon and that would be the last of us being together. She says that we're going to find our Mammy, and that when we do, everything will be just fine and we'll never be separated. She says not to speak to anyone we meet and to leave all the talking to her and to keep my mouth shut. 'If you're asked your name don't give it,' she says. And I've just to keep quiet when anybody's about.

She says we'll look in every wood in the country until we find our Mammy. And we'll keep warm at night with a good fire in places where nobody would think to look for us. She says she'll beg food at the doors of farmhouses, to keep us going with grub, and I'm not to worry about a thing. 'If they catch us we'll be split up. So do everything I tell you to do Sandy.'

If I keep a carry-on she says she'll kick my arse. If I moan when we're walking she says she'll kick my arse. And if I don't listen when she's talking she says she'll kick my arse. 'When we find our Mammy that will be the last of the homes for us,' she says. I'm in close to her now and I'm warm. She's playing with my hair. I'm tired and fall asleep.

In the morning we're up early and the sun's shining. I'm trying to write my name on the side of the wooden shed but I run out of pish. I look round and see Maggie squatting and she tells me to eff off.

I look at a farmhouse, feeling really hungry. When she's finished she looks at it too. 'Mind and keep your mouth shut,' she says, as we walk up to the door.

Maggie gives the door a good chap and it's a wee lad that answers and she tells him to go for his Mammy. It's a man with blue dungarees and a bonnet that the wee lad comes back with.

'What do you want?' he says.

'Can we get a piece from you?' Maggie asks.

'What do you want a piece for?'

A woman comes and she takes over from him.

'What do you want?' she says.

'Can we get a piece from you?' Maggie asks again.

'What do you want a piece for?'

'Because we're hungry and no had any breakfast.'

'Have you been out all night?' she asks.

'Aye.'

'Walking all night?'

'No, we slept in your shed.'

She says, 'What's your name wee boy?' but I don't answer.

'What do you want to know his name for?' Maggie asks.

'Everybody has a name. I'm Agnes, that's my husband Jimmy and the bairn's wee Jimmy.'

'I'm Maggie.'

'And who's he?'

'That's my wee brother Sandy.'

'Do you like porridge Sandy?'

'Aye, he likes porridge,' Maggie answers.

'And do you like porridge Maggie?'

'Aye.'

'Right, in you come.'

We sit at a wooden table. Wee Jimmy's about the same age as me and has a big sore at the side of his mouth and all he can do is stare.

'What are you gawking at?' I say.

'Oh you can speak,' the woman says.

'Aye.'

'Wee Jimmy's not used to visitors and he's only having a look at you.'

She brings two bowls of porridge and says there's milk and sugar if we want it. We get stuck in and the man gawks too. After a while he says he has stuff to do and pushes off.

When we're finished the woman says she'll make some toast and we can have strawberry jam that she's made herself on it. Maggie says she'll not bother with the toast and when I want some she glares at me. The woman sits at the table with us.

'So where do you stay?' she asks.

'With our Mammy,' Maggie says.

'Why were you sleeping in the shed?'

My mother as toddler, second from the left, with grandparents and great-grandparents.

Henry Reid, my father, in Boreland Wood, Fife – the camp we were taken from.

Mary Reid, my mother.

David Reid, my brother, who was killed by electrocution.

Aunt Peggy Stewart.

Left to right: Davie Stewart (my cousin), Aunt Peggy, Donald Reid (my brother) and Uncle Sandy Stewart at Lundin Links camp.

Left to right: Aunt Peggy Stewart, Uncle Sandy Stewart and Davie Stewart.

Uncle Sandy Stewart.

Aunt Peggy Stewart.

International Evangelical Gypsy Mission
Internationale Evangelische Zigeuner-Mission
Mission Evangélique Internationale Tzigane

EXECUTIVE COMMITTEE:

President:
Rev. Victor T. Hasler
Rue des Beaux-Arts 11
Neuchâtel, Switzerland

Vice-President:
Rev. Heimer Virkkunen
Mustalaislahetys r. y.
Helsinki, Finland

Treasurer:
Rev. William Webb
Blairgowrie
Perth., Scotland

Secretary:
Julius R. Feybli
Mühlestiegstrasse 44
Riehen BS, Switzerland

Travelling Secretary:
Rev. A. O. Berglund
(Rigo Lajos)
P.O. Box 621
New York 17, USA
Karlavägen 48
Stockholm, Sweden

7th September 1959.

Susan M. Beddie, S.R.N., S.C.M.,
Children's Officer,
Fife County Council,
Children's Department,
County Buildings,
Cupar, Fife.

Dear Miss Beddie,

Mrs Reid, 72 King Street, Dundee.

SMB/MG

I am writing in connection with the above Mrs Reid
who desires the return of her children who are in
your care.

For many years I have known this family and have seen
the sordid drunken behaviour of the parents in the past,
which rebounded in the suffering of their children.
I am now glad to report that with regard to the mother
of the children a miracle has happened. She has now
forsook her drunken evil ways, and for the past eleven
months has never touched liquor. In brief, she is now
a professing Christian, attends services in a Gospel
Mission in Dundee, and yesterday I had the great joy
of baptising her publicly in Dundee Baths. She has now
a four apartment house for which she has already paid
£57 and is regularly paying the instalments. I have
visited her and seen the house which in itself is a
credit to her. I can with full confidence recommend
that Mrs Reid should have her children returned to her,
and needless to say we will help her in every way.

Now, with regard to the father of the children I regret
I cannot give such a favourable report, nevertheless,
he has improved in his drunken habits and even attends
the Mission with her at times.
Without any doubt I would now say, that Mrs Reid is
capable of holding her own and caring for her children

My mother, Mary Reid, never gave up the fight to get her children back,
as this letter shows.

'Our Mammy had to go some place and she told us to wait in the shed until she came back.'

'And where did your Mammy go?'

Maggie gets up from the table and I do the same.

'We're going now,' she says, and I follow her to the door. We get to the dirt track and Maggie starts running and I run too. We get to the main road and she's flat out and I'm trying to keep up when a police car arrives.

'For fuck sake!' she shouts.

Maggie grabs my arm and hauls me over a dyke. We tear across a field and when a policeman shouts for us to stop we pay no heed. When we reach a wood my heart's pounding. We look back and they're still after us. We run down a slope, cross a burn, get through a barbed wire fence and into another field. It's neeps they have in this field and I can hardly run for the mud that sticks to my shoes. Then we're over a gate and in a lane, then through a hedge that's so thick we're scratched to bits.

'Fucking hell that was close,' Maggie says.

'Aye.'

'They'll no catch us now Sandy.'

'No.'

Maggie takes off her shoes and throws her wet socks away and I do the same. 'It was that wee man with the bonnet that got the police,' she says.

'Aye.'

'I never liked the look of that man and knew he was up to something the minute he buggered off.'

'Aye.'

'He was away to clipe,' she says.

'Aye.'

'You've no to trust anyone Sandy!'

'No.'

'Nobody bar me!'

'Aye.'

'C'mon we'll get going.'

She's in front and I'm behind. We see a big house with out-buildings and Maggie says we'll keep to the trees and make our way round to them. When we get there we have a good look round.

I see an old fashioned tractor and get myself in the driver's seat. 'Get off that thing,' she says. We wander about and there's a dose of old stuff to look at. Maggie's looking in a shed when a collie dog appears and starts barking at me.

'Shut up,' I shout, but the thing won't stop. Maggie throws a stone at it, misses, and the silly bugger fetches it and drops it back at her feet. She says if it keeps up the barking someone will come to see what's going on. She throws the stone again, and it brings it straight back and it's still barking like mad.

She was right about attracting attention and a bandy-legged man comes.

'What are you up to?' he says.

'We're just having a look about,' Maggie says.

'This is private property!'

'Aye.'

A woman comes and tells him to catch us because the police are looking for two bairns. The man grabs me and Maggie picks up a stick and threatens to bash out his brains. The man pays no heed so she whacks him in the kneecap and that's me loose.

'You wee bastards!' he shouts as we take to our heels.

We run past the house and down the drive and the collie dog's right with us. We stop at the gates and the thing's still barking so Maggie gives it a kick in the pus. We see the wee bandy man coming down the drive and the dog runs to meet him because it's finished with us now.

We've been walking a while and come to a place called the Milton Of Balgonie. We're crossing a bridge and meet an old woman. 'Have you a sixpence to spare?' Maggie asks her.

The woman gives us a look then goes in her message bag to find her purse. We get to a wee shop and Maggie has two bars of chocolate in her pocket before we get to the counter. She buys a box of matches then we're on the road again.

We come to a castle that sits in a field of cows. We're over to have a look and the place is falling to bits. We gather sticks and get a fire going and sit on rocks that have fallen from the building. She looks at me and laughs.

'You're caked with dirt,' she says.

'Aye.'

'And no socks on your feet!'

'You're the same,' I say.

'You're blacker than me,' she says.

We laugh then look for more sticks.

We're good enough in this place and have a good blaze going and the old castle walls stop the wind from cutting us.

'Do you know where our Mammy is Maggie?'

'We'll find her.'

'But do you know where she is?'

'I said we'll find her. There's a dose of places she can be Sandy.'

'What will she say when she sees us?'

'She'll be pleased to see us.'

'Will she be raging at us for running away?'

'No.'

'Will she put us back to the home Maggie?'

'No!'

'How do you know?'

'Because I do.'

'But how do you know?'

'Because I do!'

'Tell me how?'

'Shut your pus!'

She hands me a bar of chocolate and I rip the paper off and

stuff it in my mouth. When I'm finished I pester her until she gives me half of her chocolate as well. We look about the place and see two men standing at a fence. They climb over it and start walking towards us.

'Will we run Maggie?'

'No, they're no policemen.'

'What do they want?'

'Shut up!'

'What do you think they want Maggie?'

'Shut up Sandy!'

One's a big baldy man with a red face and it's him that speaks first.

'What are you doing here?' he asks.

'Just mucking about,' Maggie says.

'That's a dangerous building. You can get hurt in there!'

'Aye, but we keep out it,' she says.

'Don't tell lies, I know fine you were in there. And why have you lit a fire?'

'Because we're cold,' Maggie says.

'Where are you from lassie – how come you're not at the school?'

'We have the day off.'

'Do you now?'

'Aye.'

'Another lie!' he says, and grabs Maggie by the arm and the other one gets a grip of me. We're marched across the field and they have a car waiting near the gate. We're put in the back seat and the baldy man sits between us. He says they're policemen and that a dose of police have been looking for us all through the night. He asks why we ran away, but me and her just keep quiet and say nothing to him.

Back at the home the matron's waiting with the rest of the staff. The other bairns are at the school and the place is quiet. We've to sit on the wooden bench outside the office while the matron talks to the police. When they leave the matron takes Maggie in the office and I'm taken to the dormitory. I've to strip for a bath to get the dirt off me and it's about six inches of cold water I've to sit in. Two of them scrub me then put me in clean clothes.

I'm back on the bench and Maggie comes out the office. I'm told to wait where I am and the matron along with two staff take my sister along the corridor. I'm left sitting with nothing to do and I'm worried about Maggie. I look down the corridor but can't see or hear anything. I go halfway down and I can hear a carry-on in the girls' dormitory. Maggie's refusing to strip for a bath and they're shouting at her.

One of the staff marches me back up the corridor to sit on the bench again. This time she stands next to me so I can't go anywhere and in five minutes the matron's back. She takes me in the office and the other woman comes in too. She starts to lecture me, but I pay her no heed. She goes on about the police searching for us all night and how nobody could get to their beds because we were missing. I see the leather strap on her desk and I know that Maggie must have got a few whacks.

'Did Maggie get the belt?'

'You're not listening to a word I'm saying Sandy Reid!' She picks up the strap and puts it back in the drawer.

'Did you hit Maggie?'

'What happened to Maggie is none of your business!'

'Will I be getting it – are you going to hit me?' Then I laugh. I don't care. They just look at me and I look at them. 'Why were you shouting at my sister?' I'm still laughing. 'You hurt my sister!' I stop laughing. My voice is raised, I'm angry and I don't care what they think or what they do in this place any more. I walk out and slam the door behind me.

I go to the playroom and after a while Maggie comes and sits on a chair next to me. She has nothing to say and we just sit quiet. The wee bairns come to watch the television. We're called back to the office and the matron tells us that the Welfare's coming to see us. When we're back in the playroom Andy Pandy's just finishing up and another thing comes on the telly. It's about a grown man that runs about in a pair of short trousers like me, and that man tries to be funny and make you laugh, but I think he's just rubbish.

We sit for ages and when Miss Black finally arrives she never bothers with me and just takes Maggie away in the car. I ask the matron where she's going with Maggie and she says Miss Black wants to talk to her in private. I ask why Miss Black doesn't want to talk to me in private and she tells me to be quiet and walks away. I'm left sitting until the other bairns come in from school.

By the time Maggie's back in the place we've all had our tea. I ask her where she's been and what happened with the Welfare and she won't tell me anything. I want to know what Miss Black was saying to her and I ask why she never bothered to take me out in the car with them. I follow her about the place and torment the life out of her until she's sick of me and finally tells me what it was all about.

She says they had to check to see if she'd been near any boys when we were away. I ask what she means and she tells me Miss Black had taken her to see a doctor. She tells me she had to be checked out by the doctor, and that she had to take her pants down, and that the doctor was a man and she was embarrassed. Miss Black said if she hadn't run away she wouldn't need to have this done. She tells me she hates the Welfare, she hates the doctor, and she hates the home. She's crying now.

I go to the matron and ask why my sister had to be checked by the doctor and she tells me to go away. I ask some of the staff and they have nothing to say about it. I go back to Maggie and say it was the matron's fault. She says it was nothing to do with the matron and that it was all Miss Black's fault because she made her do it. My sister's only eleven and she has to get an examination to see if she was with a boy when we ran away. I was the only boy she was with and if Miss Black had thought to ask me I would have told her that.

They can do what they like to my sister. They can shout at her until they're hoarse. They can slap her until their hands are stinging. But they can't shame her. I won't let them shame her! I'm really angry about what's happened.

The matron's up a step-ladder fixing a light bulb. I'm still raging and run over to pull it from under her – and what a crack her leg makes when she hits the stone floor! I hadn't meant for that to happen. I just wanted to get her back for what she's put Maggie through. It's just not fair.

Ovenstone

I'm standing outside watching what goes on in this place. I can see nurses going about and I think it's maybe some kind of hospital I'm in. You only have eight bairns in this place and half of them are away home to their people for the summer holidays. I have my back to the stone wall of the wash house and it's a good sunny day in July. Three bairns are playing in a sandpit and I'm standing on my own.

'Are you no going to play with the other bairns?' It's a wee cross-eyed woman that asks me this and she tells me her name's Nelly. She's as old as the hills and says she does the washing in this place. She has a fag in her mouth and puts a match to it. You must have come in last night, she says. I just keep quiet and pay no attention to her and when she's finished her fag she buggers off.

It's a big enough building for the amount of bairns they keep, and the whole place is surrounded by fields and woods. This is much better than the town and I feel good about being back in the countryside. But I feel bad about being separated from my sister. It's my first day in this place, it's July, the sun's shining, it's my birthday and I'm nine years old. Things had got bad in Greenbanks so they've finally done the worst thing they could do and moved me to a different place from Maggie. Now I've got no one and it's the worst birthday I've ever had.

At midday they ring a bell and that means it's time for lunch. One of the nurses tells me to come and eat and it's mince and tatties they put down for us, with apple pie and custard to follow. The grub's not bad and once it's finished we're back outside and I'm sitting on a stone step when this lad with buck teeth comes over to me.

'What's the name of this place we're in?' I ask him.

'Ovenstone.'

'Where is this place?'

'I don't know.'

'How long have you been here?'

'I don't know.'

'Is this a hospital?'

'I don't know.'

This lad doesn't know much so I walk away. I go down past the washhouse and he follows at the back of me. I ask him what he wants and he doesn't answer. The other two lads are playing with a bat and ball and when one of the nurses throws the ball one of the lads whacks it right up in the air and it goes over my head. 'Get that,' I say to the lad, but he never bothers his arse and just follows me across the grass and down to the fence at the bottom of the place where you have a big concrete fort next to a wood. I'm looking at this fort and he says if you go through the fence and step over a ditch then that will get you inside the fort. I get in and sit on the wall and he's next to me. He tells me his name's Michael and that everyone calls him Rabbit. I ask why they call him Rabbit and he points to his teeth. I'm watching the lads with the bat and ball and missing my sister and wondering what this place is all about. I'm thinking maybe they're just angry with me for pulling the steps from under the matron and that I'll be back in Greenbanks once they get another matron for the place. I hate the thought of going back to Greenbanks, but I would rather be in Greenbanks with my sister than anywhere else without her.

132

The other lads get fed up with the ball game and come to sit with us. Two nurses follow at the back of them. You have a fat nurse and a thin nurse and the thin one sits on the wall, and the fat one moans about the nettles. 'I'm nurse Kate,' she says to me.

'Aye.'

'And that's nurse Jenny getting stung by all the nettles.'

'Aye.'

'And you're Sandy?'

'Aye.'

She tells me that the matron wants to see me and that I've to come up to the office with her. We go up to the building and she knocks on the office door. We go in and the matron's sitting at her desk. She's older than the matron at Greenbanks and this matron has glasses and grey hair that's tied up in a bun. She tells me I'm in Ovenstone and that this is where I'll be staying for a while. I ask if it's a hospital I'm in and she says no. I say how come you have nurses in this place and she says that's just the uniform that they wear.

Next I ask about my sister and I want to know when I will be seeing her again. She says that she'll arrange for Maggie to visit me soon and that it won't be long until I see her. She asks me what I like to do and when I tell her that I like to light fires she shudders. She tells me she's heard all about my fires and that there will be no fires in this place. If you're caught with matches you'll be in deep trouble she says. She tries to be strict when she says this but her threats mean bugger all to me. She asks what else I like to do and when I can't think of anything she says, 'I hear you like to play the piano and that you were getting lessons at Greenbanks.' She tells me they have an old piano in this place and that if I'm well behaved she'll see about getting lessons again for me.

She tells me that on Monday Dr Carlyle will be in to see me and that he'll sort out my medication for me. She says that pills will put a stop to the bad temper tantrums I'd been having in Greenbanks. She says temper tantrums hurt other people. They hurt the staff, they hurt other children and more importantly they hurt yourself. A bad-tempered child is an unhappy child she says, and we want you to be happy here in Ovenstone. She tells me that there will be no school in the place for the next four weeks because it's the holiday time. So I'll not be meeting the teachers, Miss Shepherd and Miss Kelly, until the lessons start again. She says to behave myself and I'll be just fine in this place and that things will go well for me. 'Now have you anything you want to ask me?' she says.

'Aye.'

'What?'

'Do you think my sister will send a card to me?'

'Your sister can write to you any time she likes Sandy.'

'Aye, but I want a card from her.'

'I'm sure she'll write soon.'

'Will she write today?'

'You'll have to give her time.'

'Aye, but I want a card today!'

'Sometimes you can't have everything you want straight away. You'll just have to wait and see, but I'm sure your sister will write to you soon.'

When I'm finished with the matron, Rabbit's back to me. 'We're going up to the reservoir. Are you coming?' he says.

'Aye, where is it?'

'Over there.' He points beyond some cottages.

'Are you allowed to go?'

'Aye, they don't bother what we do. Sometimes a nurse might come, other times we just go ourselves.'

There's a row of cottages across from the place and further on you have a path that takes you through a wood and up to the reservoir. We walk along by the burn – me, Rabbit, Tommy and Jack. The water comes down from the reservoir and I can see brown trout darting about in the clear pools. I feel good, and if my sister was here, I would feel even better. We come to the end of the path and the other lads start to gather stones and I ask what they're for.

'They're for the ducks!' Tommy says and in a flash they're over the hill and launching the stones at anything that floats. The ducks are frantic and trying desperately to get in the air and the boys are pishing themselves laughing. 'Look – a swan!' Jack shouts, firing off another stone.

'Missed!' Tommy whoops.

We walk round the reservoir to the other side. 'Wow, did you see that!' Jack shouts, when a big fish leaps out the water. It looks like there's a good dose of fish in this reservoir and they're jumping all over the place and some of them are a good size too. The grassy slope is neatly cut and I wonder what's at the top of it. I walk up, it's quite steep, but turns out to be worth the effort. It's another reservoir you have up here and I sit down on the grassy bank to look. The water's calm and the ducks that fled from the lower reservoir are up here now. I can see a grey heron standing with its eyes fixed on the water. I look round and the other lads are coming up the slope now. They stand beside me. 'Look at that big bird,' Jack says.

'That's a heron,' I say.

'Is it?'

'Aye.'

'What does it do?'

'It goes after wee fish.'

'What for?'

'To eat them.'

'I've seen that bird before,' he says.

'Aye, it sticks close to the water where it can catch fish.'

'Do you think it will catch a fish?'

'If it sees one, it'll grab it,' I say.

We wait, but the heron just stands like a statue and does

bugger all. After about ten minutes we get fed up waiting and walk further along the bank. Jack says we'll go up to Carnbee. I ask where that is and he points to some houses at the top of a hill about a mile away.

We walk up a wee road and it's a good enough road with hedgerows. I see two horses in a field, a white one and a black one, but it looks like the horses have had dealings with these lads before and they wander off before we get to them. A big house sits back from the road.

'That's the minister's house,' says Jack.

'It's him that takes the church on a Sunday,' says Tommy.

'You have to go to the church here?'

'Aye, we go to two churches,' Jack says. 'One week we're at the church in Carnbee and the next week we're at the church in Arncroach.'

'And you've to wear a kilt for the church!' Tommy puts in.

'A kilt!'

'Aye.'

We walk up a hill and a wee sign tells me that this is Carnbee. I look about and there's not much to the place at all. You have two or three cottages, a wee school, and further along you have a church. We walk to the church and the old iron gate creaks when we open it. There's a dose of old grave-stones in this place and I look at them and read the names of all the dead people. Some of the stones are lying on the grass, others are crumbling and look decrepit and I think the folk that looked after them probably have their own stones now. We bugger about for a while and Tommy opens the church door. Jack says he'd better not go in the place because the matron says you only need to be in the church on a Sunday and at all other times you should stay out the place. We leave the graveyard and Jack pulls the iron gate shut.

Next we wander along the road to Arncroach. What a view you have from up here. You can see all the way down to the coast and further yet. The Bass Rock sits out in the ocean and you can look right across the water and see the places on the other side. Halfway along this road sits a castle and Tommy says we'll go and have a look at the place. We go through a farm where a man's working on a tractor, but he pays us no heed and we continue down a brae that takes us into the castle grounds. Jack tells me that the man who keeps this place never bothers if you have a look about and that the name of the place is Kellie Castle.

We're sitting on the grass and Tommy's having a pee when a woman comes along on a message bike. 'You shouldn't be doing that there,' she roars at Tommy. Rabbit tells me that woman goes to the church every Sunday and that you want to hear her sing. She takes her voice that high that you would think she's was trying to put the church windows in he says.

I have a good look at these lads now. Rabbit's a quiet boy and never has much to say. Jack's finger is never out his nose and he's one of those lads that eats what he picks. And Tommy, well he's not right in the head. But they're good enough lads and I'm fine with them. When we're fed up with the castle we start back for Ovenstone.

When we get there it's different staff that are in the place. A woman comes up to me and says she's the staff nurse and that everyone calls her Staffie and that I've to do the same. She's a friendly enough woman with long black hair that's tied up. She says it's nearly tea time and that we should go and wash our hands because we can't eat our tea when our hands are dirty. If you eat your tea with dirty hands you'll get dirty germs she says and dirty germs can give you a sore belly or even make you sick enough to be laid up in your bed. If one of you gets sick then you can all get sick and then we'll have a place full of sick people she says, and we can't have that, so go and wash your hands. We clean ourselves up then go to the dining room and it's macaroni and cheese for eating. With the fresh air and walking we've done we're starving and wolf it down quickly. After that you can have bread and jam and a biscuit if you like, and there's no regulations about what way you take your food in this place. If you want a biscuit before a piece that's fine and you can drink your milk as you eat your grub, and there's no set order for putting things in your mouth like there was in Greenbanks.

We're ready to go and Staffie tells us all to wait. These lads don't like to hang about after their grub and start to moan. One of the nurses comes walking in with a big birthday cake. 'It's Sandy's birthday today,' Staffie says, and they all sing Happy Birthday to me. I blow out the candles on the cake, and when Staffie puts down some presents I'm quick to rip them open. I get a bow and arrow set, a machine gun that has sparks flying out the end of it when you pull the trigger and some sweets. One of the nurses cuts the cake and we all get a bit. I have two birthday cards and I know who one of them will be from. 'This will be from my sister,' I say, as I open the first. I read it and it says happy birthday Sandy from all the staff at Ovenstone. I toss it on the table and pick up the other card. 'This one has to be from my sister,' I say. But it says happy birthday Sandy from all the boys in Ovenstone. I ask if there's any more cards for me and when Staffie says no I bugger off. I hope Maggie hasn't forgotten about me already.

You only have one nurse on at night and she sleeps in a room between the two dormitories. There are seven beds in my dormitory and the wee lassie that lives in the place must have a dormitory all to herself. The nurse that's on this night never bothers if you talk in your bed like they did at Greenbanks. They have different rules here and if you talk in your bed you don't have to stand on a stone floor in your bare feet for hours. You're allowed to talk for as long as you like in this place. The boys fall asleep and when they're snoring I think about my sister.

I get up and go to the bathroom. I don't bother with the light and when I'm finished I look out the window. It's dark, but I can still make out the fields and woods in the moonlight. All I can do is think about my sister and I'm really missing her now. I wonder if she's awake and thinking about me the way I'm thinking about her. I wish the Welfare hadn't separated us and I wish we were still together. Maybe if I was to give a promise never to pull a step-ladder from under the matron again then I might be allowed back to Greenbanks to be with Maggie again. I think maybe they've just put me in this place to give me a fright and to make me behave and follow the rules that they want you to live by.

I hear the nurse coming but I don't bother to get down from the window. She asks me why I can't sleep and I tell her that I miss my sister. She says to go back to my bed and she comes and sits with me. She says we should whisper so that we don't waken the other lads and I talk to her about Maggie and she listens. I tell her that I miss her and that I want to be with her and she says that the matron is going to arrange for Maggie to visit me soon. She says I can come into her room if I like and she'll make me a cup of cocoa and that I'll feel better if I drink that, and it will help me to sleep.

It's just a wee room she has with a single bed and a chest of drawers. She makes the cocoa and brings it to me. 'Just sip it because it will be hot,' she says.

'I think Maggie's glad I'm in this place,' I say.

'What makes you think that Sandy?'

'I tormented the life out of her. And maybe she got fed up with me and asked the Welfare to shift me away from her. So she could get some peace.'

'You'll see her soon Sandy.'

'No, that's us split up now and I don't think I'll see her again.'

'Of course you'll see her again.'

139

I don't bother with the cocoa and put it down. I ask the nurse how long she thinks it will be until Maggie gets to visit me and she says she'll tell the matron that I'm really missing her bad. Then I tell her that Maggie never sent me a birthday card.

Doctor Carlyle is a fat man with a silver beard and a silver pocket watch. It's a good watch he has and it dangles on a chain so that he can't lose it. I ask to have a look at it and he hands it over. He tells me to press a pin at the top and when I do it flips open and you can see what time it is. I'm looking at this watch and he's sitting in his chair smiling. I ask him what he's smiling about and he says that he's just a happy man and I say that's good because I'm not a happy boy. When he asks why I'm unhappy I tell him that I miss my sister.

I ask him when my sister will be coming to visit me and he says that they're trying to arrange a visit. I ask if I'll be going back to Greenbanks and he says that I won't be. I give him one more chance to come up with a day when my sister will visit me and when he can't do that I leave the office.

The pills they put me on are orange and you're not sup-posed to bite them. I bite them and the liquid inside has a hor-rible taste. They're supposed to calm you down and stop you having bad temper tantrums. But I've not been having any temper tantrums in this place, so I ask the matron why I have to take them. She says that they're good for me and that I'll feel better after I take them. They give me medication three times a day and some of the other lads have to take pills as well. You've got different pills for different boys and they seem to know what pill suits what boy and how many pills each boy needs to take.

There are two staff nurses in the place and one of them is a man. His name's Mister Watson and he's as bald as a coot and wears glasses with black rims. I've noticed that this man's good with his hands and I've seen him sorting out Rabbit and Jack a few times. He grips them by the arm and skelps their arse hard and keeps at it until his hand gets sore with dishing out the slaps, and then he stops. He never bothers with me, but I'll be keeping a close eye on him, and if he wants to give me a few slaps he'll need to catch me first.

One day he's sitting on the stone steps at the front of the building with a fishing rod in his hands. 'Are you going fishing?' I say.

'Aye,' he says.

'That's a good enough fishing rod you have there. Do you catch much fish with it?'

'Aye,' he says.

I walk away and he calls me back. He asks me if I'd like to have a go at the fishing and says that he has a spare rod in his van if I'm interested. I tell him that I'll have a think about it and he goes to the van and gets the rod anyway. He's back quick and hands the rod to me and I have a look at it. I decide to give it a try and say that I'll go fishing with him to see what it's all about. He says I'll need to fix up the line first and put a spool on the rod and tie hooks on the end of the gut before I can try for a fish. He says if I sit long enough he'll show me what to do. So I sit, and he shows me.

When we're done he says that we'll need to get some bait to put on the hooks. We go to the garden and he turns the earth over with a spade and tells me to pick up every worm I see and put them in a jar. When we have a dose of worms he says that's us set to go fishing now. I ask if Rabbit and Jack will be coming with us and he says that it will just be me and him that go fishing and that the other lads can find something else to do.

The place where he wants to fish is about two miles from Ovenstone. You've to go up past Arncroach to get to this reservoir and it sits halfway up a hill and the name of the place is Gillingshill. You've to be careful where you put your feet in this place because it's a steep bank you've to get down. The stones at the water's edge are covered in green slime, and you've to be careful that you don't slip and bash your brains out.

This man's keen to catch a fish and gets started right away. I just take my time and have a good look round the place while he sets up his rod. He gathers the line and puts a worm on the hook then throws the line in the water. He says to keep my eye on the float for him while he goes for a pish. 'If that float goes under the water let me know quick,' he says. He's behind a bush when the float bobs up and down and I roar that he has a fish. This man's quick to react, and near sets his neck when he slips on the slime and batters his arse on the stones. He's back on his feet quick and near in a panic, so I tell him to calm down or he'll land himself in the water with all his excitement. He gets a grip of the rod and gives it a jerk and tells me that he has a good fish on the hook. The rod's near bent in two with the weight of that fish, and he thinks he might have a good fight on his hands too. He tells me to keep quiet so that he can concentrate on getting this fish ashore.

You've to play the fish and that takes a good bit of skill that he says he's got. I watch as he winds the spool slowly. Then he gives the line a bit more slack and lets the fish run about for a while. He says that if you keep that up for long enough then the fish will eventually tire itself out and that's when you can land it and see what like a fish it is. It's a fit fish he has on that hook and after a while the line goes slack.

'I think you've lost your fish.'

'I've not lost the fish,' he says.

'Aye you have.'

'No I've not – it's resting!' he says.

'Well pull it in!'

'You can't just pull a fish in, you've to take your time, and play it.'

'I would just pull it in.'

'This is not your fish Sandy! When you have your own fish on your own line then you can pull it in as quick as you like.'

He's taking forever and when I tell him that I would have landed that fish by now he tells me to shut up. I'm watching and the line's still slack and I think that the fish is off the hook. Suddenly it leaps in the air and lands back in the water with a big splash and the fight's back on. After a while he tells me that he has the fish under control and that he'll have it on the bank soon. He's quicker winding the spool this time and soon I get my first look at the fish as he brings it nearer to the shore. He's down on his knees and has his hand out ready to grab it when it gives one last jerk. And that's it off the hook and it buggers off.

'Fuck!' he says.

'That fish was too fly for you,' I say.

He sorts out his line and puts another worm on the hook and casts out again. 'Are you going to try for another one now?'

'Aye,' he says.

I just leave my rod sitting where it is because I'm not ready to try for a fish yet and I go for a wander round the place. He tells me to watch what I'm doing because the stones are slippy and he should know because he's already been on his arse. He says if I fall in and get tangled in the weeds then he would have a job to get me out. So if I land in the water I might drown.

I go along a bit to where there's grass and it's easier to walk. A platform juts out in the water like a wee bridge and you can walk out and look straight into the water from here. I see a few fish going about and I shout to him that he's fishing in the wrong bit. I make my way round to the opposite bank, but he just sits where he is and pays no heed to my advice. I climb onto a big boulder that has a flat top and this looks a good spot to try for a fish.

I'm back to him for my rod and he puts a worm on the hook for me. 'Where are you going to fish?' he says.

'On top of that rock.'

'Watch where you're putting your feet and pay attention because I don't want to be fishing you out the water.'

I'm back to my bit and gather up the line and cast out. Then I sit and wait. I look about and it's a quiet peaceful place you have here. All you can hear are birds singing, and maybe the splash of a fish now and again. I leave my rod sitting and go for a wander. When I get back to Mr Watson he has his nose in a book. 'What's that you're reading?' I ask. He shows me the cover and it has a picture of a big fish on the front. I think that book teaches the man how to fish properly and maybe he's trying to find out what he did wrong when he lost that fish earlier.

I'm back to pick up my rod and start to reel it in slowly. Suddenly there's a mighty tug on the line and I've got a fish hooked. He's up quick and on his way to me. He's shouting instructions and giving advice about what to do and what not to do. But I just reel this fish in as fast as I can. He tells me to take it easy and not to reel so quick or I'll lose the fish, but I pay him no heed and wind that spool at a hundred miles an hour. This fish gets no time to run about and tire itself out the way his did. And before you can blink I have it out the water and dangling on the end of my line. It's shaking and wriggling to get off that hook, so I jerk the rod straight up in the air and it soars over my head and the line snaps. I look behind and see the fish flapping about in the long grass and I'm over quick to give it a good stamp with my foot.

'That's no way to kill a fish!' he shouts, but I pay him no heed and give it another few stamps. 'You'll squash that fish!' he roars, but I'm not bothered about squashing the thing, because I'm trying to kill it. Then he's over and gets it by the neck and tears the hook out its mouth. It's wriggling about in his hands, and what a size it is.

144

'That's about four pound. That's a good fish you have Sandy!'

'Aye.'

'I'll need to kill it humanely,' he says, as he grabs it by the tail and batters its brains out on the end of his Welly boot. It's a good few whacks this fish needs to stop it living and when he's finished doing that he throws it in the long grass and the thing's still twitching yet. He tells me it's a really good fish and that it would do for his tea and that it's a rainbow trout I have there. He picks it up again and shows me the colours of the rainbow running along its side. 'That's why it's called a rainbow trout,' he says.

I've only seen wee brownies before and this was the first rainbow trout I'd seen in my life. He said I must be really pleased with myself for that was a good fish to catch and he asks if I'm going to try for another. I tell him that I'll just sit and watch him now. We're at this reservoir for a few more hours but he catches bugger all and it's just the one fish that we have to go back to Ovenstone with. I think he's disappointed that he never managed to catch a fish and I tell him that if he keeps reading his book and heeds its advice he'll land a rainbow himself one day.

When we're back in the place I show my fish to Rabbit and Jack. Next I show the nurses, then it's the matron's turn to see it.

I walk in the office and slap the fish on the matron's desk and she shudders.

'Get that fish off my desk!' she roars.

'It won't touch you – it's dead!' I say.

'I don't care how dead it is – get it off my desk!'

I tell her to calm down, and when she does, she says it's a good enough fish but she's not happy about it being on her desk. She says the cook would be the best person to show that fish to and when I hold it up for her to get a better look she shudders again. 'Get out of my office and take that fish with you!' she shouts.

I go to the kitchen and find the cook. She likes the trout and says that it would look good on a plate once she's cooked it. I tell her she can have the fish, but I've still to show it to a few more people first. From the kitchen I go to the washhouse and Nellie thinks it's a good fish. The gardener thinks it's a good fish too and says it's a big fish to catch on your first fishing trip. I tell him that there's bigger fish than that to be caught at Gillingshill and that I'll be going back to catch a bigger one yet. After a while I've had enough of the fish so I hand it to the cook and tell her to keep it.

I'm a month in the place and it's not bad. My lessons start today and my sister will be visiting at the weekend. It's my first time in this classroom and it's nothing like the classroom I was in at Parkhill. We all sit round a table with the teachers, Miss Shepherd and Miss Kelly. It's a big enough classroom and there's bits where you can go to paint or mess about with plasticine to make models and stuff like that. The classroom has big enough windows and if you're bored with your lessons you can look out them to keep your mind occupied.

Miss Shepherd says we'll practise counting and she starts with the two times table and works her way right up to the twelve times table. We get out for our lunch and in the afternoon we listen to a nature programme on the wireless. Miss Kelly goes on about the nature programme for a bit then that's your lessons over for the day. Most of the bairns are in the class every day but some don't bother much with their lessons and just bugger off when they're called to the classroom. But I've put in the whole week at my lessons because that's one of the conditions they've made for my sister getting to visit me at the weekend.

At last it's Saturday afternoon and a green Hillman Imp

146

comes in the place. I'm waiting on the stone steps and watch the Greenbanks matron get out the car along with my sister and two wee lassies.

'I see your leg's fixed Matron.'

She pays me no heed and hobbles up the stone steps.

'Sandy!' It's my sister.

'Maggie!' I'm beaming from ear to ear.

'Hello Sandy,' a wee lassie says.

'What do you two want?' I ask.

'The matron brought them two along to fill the car,' Maggie says.

'Aye, well, I don't want to see them. It's you I want to see Maggie.'

We walk down to the woods and the wee lassies follow.

Maggie notices my irritation at this intrusion. 'Never mind them Sandy,' she says.

'Don't go far,' the Ovenstone matron shouts after us.

We go in the fort. Maggie and I sit on the wall and the wee lassies stand gawking.

'What are you looking at?'

'Never mind them Sandy,' Maggie says.

'What are they doing here?'

'We've come to visit you too,' one lassie says.

'Aye, well you can bugger off!'

The two lassies move away and Maggie says, 'Do you like this place Sandy?'

'Aye, it's better than Greenbanks.'

'You have woods here. Do they let you run about in them?'

'Aye.'

'I wish I was here with you.'

'I wish you were here too Maggie.'

'I hate Greenbanks!' she says.

'Can you no ask the Welfare to put you in here with me then Maggie?'

'They'll no do that Sandy.'

'How no?'

'They just won't.'

I lower my voice. 'Do you want to run away again Maggie? We can bugger off right now.'

'I don't think we should do that Sandy.'

'How no?'

'Because they would put a stop to my visits if we did that.'

'Aye, but we wouldn't get caught this time.'

'We're better to behave ourselves Sandy. That's the only way I'll get to keep the visits up to you.'

'Aye, ok.'

Maggie's visit lasted an hour and then it was time for her to go back to Greenbanks. I stood waving at the road end and wondered how long it would be until she was allowed to visit me again and I felt sad. But I knew why they had separated us – it was because I was bad. I only had to behave and all would be well. At least that's what I thought. But, how wrong I was. Miss Black had already made plans for Maggie – plans that would take her far, far away from me.

I'm sitting on the grass at the back of the place when one of the nurses shouts for me. She has a man with her that I've never seen before. She tells me he's a music teacher and that he's going to take over my piano lessons. I get in his car and he drives me to his house in Pittenweem. When we get there he takes me into a room and I look at his piano. He says to have a shot on the thing while he gets himself a cup of tea. It's a long time since I played the piano and I just bugger about with the keys and play a wee tune to myself. When he's back he just sits in a chair and watches me.

I ask him if he wants a shot and he says he's happy to just sit and listen to me. I get off the stool and look out the window. He puts down his tea and plays a tune and when he's finished

I tell him that he's a good piano player. This seems to give the man more confidence and he plays a better and longer tune.

When he's finished I'm back on the stool and he starts me off on the scales. He shows me the right way to hold my hands and how to do the scales properly. I've already done this stuff before but my fingers are rusty and he says when I get back to Ovenstone I should practise on the old piano that they have in that place.

They want to do a test to see if I'm right in the head. You have to go to Edinburgh for this test and they say I can pick a toy from a toy shop and have my tea in a fancy restaurant and that it will be a good day out. I want the toy and I want my tea in a restaurant, but I don't want the test. Miss Black has told me that I have nothing to worry about. She says lots of children have had this test done before and that I shouldn't feel anxious about it. But I was worried out my skull and hardly slept a wink the night before.

Three of them are in the car with me and they don't have much to say. A man sits in the front with Miss Black and another man sits in the back with me. I don't know the men but she tells me they're social workers and that they're good people. She speaks to the man in the front and the one next to me just looks out the window.

'What's his name?' I ask her.

'Who's name?' she says.

'Him that's sitting next to me. What's his name?'

'Why don't you ask him yourself Sandy?'

'You ask him.'

'No,' she says.

'What's your name Mister?'

'Mister Clifford.'

It's a long journey, the furthest I've ever been in a car and it takes forever to get to the place. I don't know what this is about and nobody's saying much, so I'll just have to wait and see what happens when I get there. They're lucky it's not my sister they're taking for a test because, if it was, she would be sick in the car. The car would be smelling of sick because she would have spewed her guts up by now. It doesn't have to be a long drive in a car for Maggie to be sick. If you drove her just a wee bit up the road she would be sick. That's enough to get her going. She's sick in cars, she's sick living in Greenbanks home, and I think she's sick of me.

'Have you ever met my sister Mr Clifford?'

'No,' he says.

'Her name's Maggie.'

'That's a nice name,' he says.

The man in front turns round and offers Mr Clifford a fag. He strikes a match. 'Do you want to blow it out Sandy?'

'No.'

'You can blow it out if you like, but you'll need to be quick or I'll burn my fingers.' I just look at him and he blows it out himself and throws the match out the window.

When we're at the place we've to sit for ages until it's my turn to be seen. Mr Clifford has his nose in a book and the other man has his nose in a newspaper and Miss Black's nose is everywhere. They shout for me and we've to follow a woman for about a mile to get to the room where they want to do the test. In this room I've to lie on a doctor's bench with my feet at one end and my head at the other. The woman gets me ready for the test and slaps blobs of glue on different bits of my skull. Next she sticks pads on and there's a dose of wires all over the place. Miss Black watches, the two men watch, and I just lie there and let them get on with it and say bugger all. When they're finished I'll get to pick a toy and have my tea in a fancy restaurant and that will be good. After the test we walk back to the car. It's colder and cloudier now and the sun's gone.

Miss Black's not sure what road to take. The men have no

clue what road to take either and I don't care what road we take. After a while she says she's lost and him in the front tries to work out where we should be going and him in the back next to me sits quiet and says bugger all. I'm not bothered about being lost and tell her not to worry and just to find a toy shop. She says a toy shop's not important right now and that finding our way out of Edinburgh and back to Ovenstone is. I tell her to pay no heed to where we are and to stop at the first toy shop she comes to because I want to pick my toy. The man in front tells me to shut up and I tell him to shut up. Miss Black tells me not to be cheeky and Mr Clifford tells me to behave and I tell him to shut his pus.

She stops at a toy shop and I get a cap gun. Back in the car I'm busy loading the caps and Mr Clifford watches what I'm doing. I point the gun at him and pull the trigger. Bang! He ignores me and looks out the window.

'You can fire your caps when we get back to Ovenstone,' Miss Black says.

I pay her no heed. Bang, bang, bang.

'Will you stop firing that gun Sandy!'

Bang, bang, bang, bang, bang. Bang, bang, bang! I fire off every single cap and that's them finished now.

'Am I going for my tea now?'

'When I can find a restaurant,' she says.

'Can you open the window?'

'Are you too hot Sandy?'

I don't answer and when she opens the window I toss the gun out.

'What did you do that for?' she says.

'No caps!'

Nothing much seems to come from the test and I don't hear any more about it. And I don't ask. They can do what they like. And maybe I'm not wrong in the head after all.

* * *

I have a cricket bat and Tommy's throwing a ball to me. He throws it, I whack it, he runs to get it, then throws again, and he's happy with that. Jumbo's back in the place and he's a big lad who I've heard lots about. His Welfare woman brought him back about an hour ago and she's getting ready to leave now. We're playing on the grass as she drives out the place and Jumbo waves. She's going down the road and that boy's still waving. She goes round the bend and he stops waving.

He comes over to us. He never bothers to introduce himself and just tells me to hand over the bat. I look at him and Tommy throws the ball away and says he's fed up with the game now. Jumbo wants the bat and says if I don't hand it over he'll smack my chops. He's a big lad, big enough to kill you with his bare hands, so I've to think carefully about the best way to tackle him. Whack! I put the bat round his lug and bugger off.

I go to the kitchen and the cook asks me if I like kippers. Kippers are good for you she says – any kind of fish is good for you. She tells me fish give you brains and if you have brains you can work out problems, and if you can work out problems, then you'll never really have a problem. I try a bit of a kipper and I don't like it, so I'll just have to make do with the brains I've got.

The other lads eat their kippers and it's scrambled eggs they put down for me. When we're finished our lunch a nurse comes in with Jumbo. She says she found him wandering about in a daze and she thinks that he's maybe missing his family now that he's back in the place. Jumbo has no interest in kippers and I don't think he's tasted any kind of fish in his life. He has scrambled eggs, the same as me, and after his lunch he clipes to the matron.

The matron's not happy about things and says it was a bad thing to hit Jumbo with the bat. She says I could have killed that lad. She tells me to stop looking out the window and to listen to what she's saying. Jumbo's been checked out and he's fine and the matron wants me to say sorry to him.

'Will you apologise to him Sandy?'

'Aye.'

'When you apologise to someone you have to really mean that you're sorry.'

'Aye.'

'Are you sorry?'

'Aye.'

'Do you mean it?'

'Aye.'

'I'm going to get Jumbo now.'

'Aye.'

'And you'll say you're sorry when he comes?'

'Aye.'

'And you'll mean it?'

'Aye.'

She goes looking for Jumbo and I bugger off.

You have a cupboard full of kilts in this place and you can pick any colour you like to wear for the church. You have all different sizes and some of the kilts go down past your knees and others go up round your arse, and you've to try and pick out one that fits you fine. You have a dose of sporrans to choose from and the one I pick was likely running about a wood before it became a sporran. This week they have us to the church in Arncroach and you've to sit quiet and listen to the minister's rants for about an hour before they let you out the place.

After the service I'm outside leaning against a stone wall when a farm boy comes over to me. 'I can drive an MF and a JD,' he says.

'What's an MF and a JD?'

'They're tractors,' he says.

'Are they?'

153

'Aye, a Massey Ferguson and a John Deere.'

'And you can drive them?'

'Aye.'

'Can you drive a combine harvester?'

'No,' he says.

'How no?'

'Because it's only tractors I can drive.'

'You're no a real farmer until you can drive a combine harvester,' I say.

'How do you know – what do you know about farmers?' he asks.

'Plenty!'

He asks if I can drive a tractor and I tell him to shut his pus and bugger off.

Maggie's coming to visit me again and I'm looking forward to it. I seem to spend most of my days just wishing them away. I want every day to pass as quickly as possible, because every day that passes is one day closer to seeing Maggie again. When the Greenbanks matron drives into the place I'm waiting on the stone steps and can't wait to see my sister. The car stops beside me, but there's no sign of Maggie. A young lad gets out and says hello to me but I pay him no heed. He's followed by two wee lassies and I ignore them too. 'Where's my sister?' The matron ignores me and walks into the building. One wee lassie says that it's not Maggie's turn to visit me, and when I ask what she means by that she just looks at me.

I go straight to the office and demand to know why my sister's not here to visit me. The Greenbanks matron says it's not Maggie's turn to visit me this time. She says that all the other bairns in Greenbanks miss me just as much as Maggie does and that they have to get the chance to see me as well. I tell her that the other bairns don't interest me, and that it's my sister I want to see. I ask her to go back to Greenbanks and get my sister. But she refuses to do this and tells me that I'll just have to make do with the bairns that she's brought to see me.

I'm back outside and the Ovenstone lads are over at the washhouse with the Greenbanks bairns. The wee Greenbanks boy has a dose of scabs on his face and both the lassies are glaickit. 'What's your name?' I ask him.

'Billy,' he says. 'Do you no remember me Sandy?'

'Aye, I remember you. What are you doing here?'

'I'm visiting you,' he says.

'What are you visiting me for?'

'He put his hand up,' one of the lassies says.

'What do you mean he put his hand up?'

'The matron said to put your hand up if you wanted to visit Sandy in his new place.'

'Did she?'

'Aye.'

'And did my sister put her hand up?'

'Aye.'

'Then how come she's no here?'

'Because the matron says she got to visit you the last time.'

'So?'

'She said that other bairns should get a chance to see you.'

'Did you put your hand up?' I ask her.

'Aye,' she says.

'Well see the next time she asks you if you want to visit me, don't bother putting your hand up. Because, if I see you in this place again I'll boot your fucking arse! And that goes for the lot of you! Don't any of you put your hands up to visit me again!'

'Let's batter them,' Jumbo says, and he pushes the wee laddie on his arse. I'm raging and storm over to the garden where I lift a good stone. Then I'm back to the matron's car to put it clean through the windscreen. Two nurses and the Staffie are onto me quick and take a good hold of me.

'He's smashed my car windscreen,' the Greenbanks matron roars. And if I could get myself free, it would be her skull I'd be smashing next.

The Ovenstone matron tells her to shut up and to get out the place. 'If you'd brought his big sister to see him we wouldn't be having this carry-on!' she says.

I'm going mental now and start lashing out with my feet, but they have a good grip of me and drag me off to the dormitory. They get me down on the floor and one nurse sits on my chest, the other one sits on my legs, and the Staffie has a good grip of my hands. I'm roaring at the top of my voice and trying to kick my feet but I can't move, and they just sit where they are and pay me no heed. They have me like this until I'm hoarse with all the shouting I'm doing. I'm angry because my sister never got to visit me and I'm frustrated because I can't fucking move. I hate the Greenbanks matron. I hate all the bairns in Greenbanks. And I hate the nurses in this place too.

When I calm down I just lie, they just sit, and nothing happens.

Then matron comes. She sits on a chair and says nothing. Nobody says anything, nobody pays any attention to me. I'm knackered, and hoarse with all the shouting I've been doing. I just want to get up and bugger off but they keep me pinned to the floor.

'I need the toilet.'

No answer.

'I need the toilet!'

Still no answer.

'I need the fucking toilet!'

They pay no heed.

I turn to the matron and she's looking out the window. The nurse on my chest is looking at her nails and I can't see the one that's sitting on my legs. I'm frustrated with the whole thing. I can't move and there's bugger all I can do. I hate this place, I hate all the nurses. I hate the Greenbanks matron for not bringing my sister to visit me. I hate the Welfare woman and I hate my fucking sister too.

My eyes open and the weight's off my chest. I can move my legs, shake my arms and wriggle my fingers. It's quiet, I'm alone now and still lying on the floor. I get to my feet and go to the bathroom. I look at the stream of pish, it's cloudy and I've never seen pish like that before. My head hurts, I'm hot and so I splash cold water on my face.

I go outside and stand on the veranda where the air's cooler. I look about, no one's around, no nurses, no matron, no boys. I go to the kitchen and the cook tells me to sit at the table and she'll get me something to eat. She brings soup and I spread butter onto bread and dip it in the bowl. Two nurses come and the cook brings them cups of tea. They light fags and blow smoke rings in the air. They talk about the Beatles and pay me no heed. When my soup's finished I bugger off.

I'm sitting in the television room with the other lads and they're watching a film with the Staffie. I have no interest in the film and I'm thinking about running away. Maggie should have listened to me. We should have run away together.

'Hey you, wee boy, come here a minute.' It's the woman across the road. 'I want to speak to you,' she says.

I open the gate and walk up the path. She lives in a cottar house and I've been watching her messing about with the weeds in her garden. She's never paid me any heed before and this is the first time she's spoken to me. The man with the motorbike stays here too and I can see the bike leaning against the wall of the house.

'What's your name?' she says.

'Sandy.'

'I'm Mrs Taylor.'

'Aye.'

'I've seen you going about with some of the other lads.'

'Aye.'

She sees me looking at the bike. 'Do you like motorbikes Sandy?'

'Aye.'

'Do you like biscuits?'

'Aye.'

'Wait there. I've got some that's ready to come out the oven now.'

'Aye.'

It's a red motorbike the man has and it's gleaming. He's never done polishing that motorbike and I've seen him going at it with a cloth for hours at a time. If he's not watching the television, or eating his grub, then you'll catch him shining that motorbike up. It's every single bit that he cleans and sup-posing you never seen a speck of dirt on that bike with your own two eyes, he would spot it, and wipe it clean. And when he starts it up, what a roar you get. And when he goes down the road you would think a rocket had just flown past you. I've been at the bottom of that road, standing where the bend is, and when he's taken that bike round the corner you see him leaning right over, and it's a wonder that man's no taken his kneecap off before now. It's a black leather jacket he wears when he drives that motorbike and it's a good pair of boots he has on his feet. She's back with the biscuit and hands it to me.

'Who belongs that motorbike?' I ask.

'That's my son's bike,' she says.

'How come he only drives it in the afternoon?'

'Because he's a lazy bugger!'

'What do you mean?'

'He never gets out his bed until the afternoon.'

'If that was my motorbike I would be up early every day to drive it.'

I'm finished the biscuit when the man comes out the door.

He's got on the leather jacket and the big boots and that means he's going out on the motorbike. He pulls the bike from the wall and wheels it down the path. I watch as he takes it out the gate and onto the dirt track. I walk to the gate and he nods for me to get on the back of the thing.

'Put your arms round me and grip tight,' he says.

'Aye.'

'Are you ready?'

'Aye!'

'Get off that motorbike Sandy!' Mrs Taylor shouts, but I pay her no heed.

He kicks down the start bar but all you get is a splutter and the bike does bugger all.

'Get him off that fucking bike!' she roars.

'Hurry up and start the thing!' I shout to him.

He kicks again, and what a roar you get this time as it charges up and I can feel the vibrations right up my arse.

'Take off!' I roar.

We go haring round the countryside for what seems like ages and then we get back to where we first started. It feels amazing and my legs are like jelly when I get off. I think it's the most exciting thing I've ever done. When he drops me off, he just roars away down the road, the bike gleaming in the sun.

It's the week before Christmas and all the other bairns are getting ready to go home to their own people and it will be next year before they're back in Ovenstone. I'll be staying in this place, and not going anywhere for Christmas. But I'm hoping that they'll bring Maggie to see me. That's my Christmas wish.

I'm called to the office and the matron has news for me. She tells me that Miss Black has telephoned and asked her to pass a message to me. Maggie has been moved out of Greenbanks, far away, to a place in Aberdeen. She will not be visiting me in the near future because she will need time to settle into her new place. When I leave the office I'm thinking that that will be the last time I wish for anything in my life, because wishes don't come true. Looking back, this was the moment when everything changed for me and life changed dramatically. All decisions about me were taken by the Welfare. Where I should stay, what family members I was allowed to see, what I should eat, when I should sleep. For the first time in my life I realised that the Welfare controlled my life totally. I was not involved in any decision-making process. My fate was entirely in their hands. Soldiers talk of a 'bullet that has his name on it'. For me, I realised the bullets were being fired by the Welfare. This time it seemed to be aimed straight at my head – but I was determined to survive.

A wood is the best place in the world to clear your head, and the best place in the world to sharpen yourself up and that's where I was going now. Tommy asks to come with me and Rabbit comes too.

At the Grangemuir we raid the hen huts and smash all the eggs. When we're fed up with that we sit on a dyke dangling our feet. Tommy's excited about Christmas and excited about going home and excited about smashing the eggs. Rabbit's not excited about Christmas and not excited about going home and he's picking a scab off his knee.

'This time tomorrow I'll be home,' Tommy says.

'Aye.'

'I can do what I like at home.'

'You can do what you like here,' I say.

'Aye, but you can do what you like better when you're at home.'

We cross a field of sheep and make our way back to the Ovenstone Wood. Tommy strikes ahead and we're about halfway over the field when he comes rushing back.

'There's tinks in the wood!' he roars. 'Come and see.'

We run to the wood and follow him to a clearing where the tinks are sitting at a fire. I can see two of them, a man and a woman and they're watching us. I remember Maggie saying that if I ever came across tinks I was to go up to them and tell them my name and she said they would be just fine with me. I'm not sure about going anywhere near these people as they have a wild look about them and I'm happy to just stand and look at them for now.

'They're looking at us,' Rabbit says.

'Aye.'

'What will we do Sandy?'

'Nothing.'

'Will we just look back at them?'

'Aye, just look at them.'

'Do you think they'll chase us?'

'No.'

Tommy lets fly with a stone and it pings off an old pot and that gets the man to his feet. 'Run!' Tommy whoops, and we bolt back to the wooden gate.

'If that tinky man gets a grip of us we'll be murdered,' says Rabbit, catching his breath.

'He's an old man. He can't catch us,' Tommy says.

I'm taking deep breaths and when I look up the old man's standing there. 'Who threw that stone?' he says.

'Him!' Tommy says, pointing to Rabbit.

'I never did!' Rabbit protests.

'Aye you did, and I told him not to mister,' Tommy says.

'I'm no caring who threw it. You shouldn't be throwing stones at people. How would you like it if I was to throw stones at you?'

We've no answer to that and just stand looking at the man. It's a checked jacket he wears and a well-worn bunnet sits on his head. 'Gather some sticks for me and bring them to my camp,' he says, before walking away.

'Bugger that!' Tommy says.

'No, we'll get sticks for him,' I say.

'I'm no getting sticks for him.'

'How no?'

'Because he can get his own sticks. C'mon let's go.'

Me and Rabbit start to gather sticks and Tommy leans against the gate watching us. When we have a good bundle we take them to the tinker's camp and Tommy follows. 'Is that enough sticks for you?' I say.

'Aye, that's fine, well done lads,' he says.

We stand looking and he tells us to sit on our arses and to have a crack with him. He tells us not to worry about anything because he's not going to touch us and we'll be fine with him. We sit down and I have a good look at him now. He's a wee man, unshaved and weather-beaten. But he's friendly enough and nothing about him worries me. I look at her and she's a wee fat woman with yellow hair and matching yellow teeth. She wears a big coat and a head square. She pulls black stuff from her pocket that she cuts with a penknife. She hands a bit to him and he puts it in his mouth. Next she cuts a bit for herself and she chews on that.

'Is that liquorice?' Tommy asks.

'No, it's baccy.'

'Do you no have any fags?'

'This stuff's better than fags,' he says.

He asks where we live and we tell him we're in the Ovenstone home. Tommy tells him that he's going home for Christmas and says that Rabbit's going home too. He asks me if I'm going home for Christmas and I don't answer him. She's watching me and when she speaks to him she speaks quickly and in a low voice and I can't make out what she's saying to him. He looks at me then he's back to her with quick words and she's back to him with quicker words yet and I think it's a different language they're speaking altogether.

162

'What's your name?' he says to me.

'Sandy.'

'I told you!' she says.

'You have the same name as me,' he says.

'Aye?'

'My name's Sandy too,' he says.

'Aye.'

'I'm Sandy Stewart.'

'I'm Sandy Reid.'

'I told you who he was. I knew that was Mary's laddie the minute I set eyes on him!' she says.

'Hold on the now Peggy and I'll find out. What's your mammy's name Sandy?'

'Mary Reid.'

'Christ, I'm your own Uncle!' he roars.

'And I'm your Auntie!' she says.

She's on her feet and I'm on my feet too. I look at Tommy, then I look at Rabbit and they both look at me. The woman has a big smile on her face. 'Come here Sandy,' she says, and she has her arms out ready to cuddle me. She steps forward and I step back, startled. She looks at me and I look at her. Then I bugger off.

Back in Ovenstone the evening shift are just starting. Staffie's in charge tonight and that's good because I like her and she's good with me. It's dark by the time we get our tea and it's not the same when it gets dark early because you have to sit in the place and watch television all night and that bores me. That's what you do on the winter nights, watch television, play board games or maybe just bugger about with a pack of cards. I like the summer nights better because then you can run about and do what you like for longer and I hate the long dark winter nights because there's bugger all to do in this place in the wintertime.

When I'm lying in my bed I'm thinking about the tinks in the wood. It would be much better if Maggie was here because she would know what to do with them and she would be better at speaking to them than I am. She would know what to say to them and if they said to her that they were her Uncle and Auntie she would likely be pleased with that. I think she would have let the woman cuddle her, but I just don't know the people the way Maggie does and there's nothing I can do about that. If Maggie was here I would have things to say and she would ask them anything I wanted to know because she's good at asking for things and I'm not. Old Sandy was a good enough man and old Peggy was a good enough woman and if I see them again I'll tell them that Maggie's been moved to Aberdeen and if they can get up there then they can cuddle her if they want to. Because I'm just not ready to be cuddled by anyone yet.

I wonder what Sandy and Peggy are doing. I think they will have a good fire going and they'll be cracking away to each other. I wonder what it would be like to be in their tent when it's dark. How would they be able to see, would it just be the firelight they have because they don't have electric lights like we do in this place? There will be no television for them, or board games, or packs of cards to play with. The night will be a lot longer for them in the woods than it would be for me in this place. And, I think when I go back to see them, I'll go when it's dark just to see what it's like. I wonder where they sleep, because I don't think they would have a bed in their tent. Maybe they just lie on the ground and get stuck to the frost when the fire goes out. Tomorrow, Tommy and Rabbit will go home, and I'll be the only bairn left in this place and if I wasn't here then the nurses could go home too and they would be able to spend Christmas with their own people.

The next morning the music man comes to take me for my last lesson before Christmas. He has a wee present for me and

I have bugger all for him. It's a selection box he hands me and I break into it right away. That man just sits in his soft chair, drinks tea and looks worried. I sit on the piano stool and practise the scales in between stuffing my face with chocolate and when the lesson's over I have nothing left in the selection box, and I'm not fit for my lunch when I get back to the place with stuffing my face so much.

The Welfare comes for Tommy in the afternoon and he goes off to his own people and that leaves just me and Rabbit in the place.

'They'll come for you next,' I say to him.

'I hope not,' he says.

'Do you not want to go home?'

'No.'

'How no?'

'Because I like it better here.'

'Do you?'

'Aye.'

'Well ask the matron if you can bide here with me for Christmas and the New Year.'

'She'll no let me do that.'

'How no?'

'Because she won't.'

'Do you want me to ask for you?'

'Aye,' he says.

I go to the matron and tell her that Rabbit wants to bide in this place for Christmas and that he has no interest in his own people. I ask if he can stay here with me for the Christmas and the New Year and she says that he can't and that he has to go home whether he likes it or not.

'Did you see her?' he says, when I'm back to him.

'Aye.'

'What did she say?'

'She said you've to go home whether you like it or not.'

'Did she?'

'Aye.'

'What will I do now?'

'You'll have to go home.'

'Bugger!'

I like Rabbit and when it's time for him to go he waves to me from the Welfare man's car and I wave back to him. It's a Welfare man that Rabbit has and me and the rest of the bairns all have a Welfare woman. When he's gone I sit down on the stone steps and look about the place and there's bugger all to do and nobody to do anything with now.

At the back of four o'clock it starts to get dark and I see old Nelly coming from the washhouse. She sits down on the stone steps beside me. She says that it's a shame that I'm left in this place at Christmas time when all the other bairns are away home to their families. She says she would give me some money but that she's not allowed to give money to any of the bairns and would get into trouble if she did that. She tells me she would love to take me home to her place for Christmas, but she's not allowed to do that either. The only thing I can give you, says the wee cross-eyed woman, is a big cuddle and that gets her in trouble too. I watch her walking out the place and I'm thinking maybe I shouldn't have pushed her away like that because she was just trying to be nice when she wanted to cuddle me.

I think about Maggie. I hope she likes her new place in Aberdeen and I wonder if she thinks about me the way I think about her. I know that she won't be coming to visit me at Christmas now and that makes me feel sad. I hope she's pleased with the card that I made for her and I hope that she's remembered to send me one too. Tomorrow will be the last day for letters before Christmas and I'll be waiting to see if the postman has a card for me.

I'm up early for my breakfast and I'm waiting for the

postman now. It's a bicycle that man goes about on and sometimes you get him early and other times you get him late. This
postman's good for cracking to people and can be long
enough handing out the letters with the amount of blethering
and cups of tea that he drinks at the different houses. If you're
expecting a letter or a card you can wait long enough for him
to deliver it to you. His bike's been sitting outside Mrs Taylor's
house for a while now and it's this place he'll be at next.

'You took your time!' I say, when he arrives.

'Well it's nice to chat to people and spread a bit of
Christmas cheer,' he says.

'Aye.'

'Mrs Taylor tells me you're in this place yourself for
Christmas, Sandy.'

'Aye, have you anything for me in your mail bag?'

'Aye,' he says, handing a Christmas card to me.

I open it quick and it's a card from him to me.

'That's from you!' I say.

'Aye.'

'Have you anything else for me?'

'No, there's nothing else,' he says, so I hand the card back
and bugger off. I just can't believe that Maggie hasn't sent me
a card.

I'm sitting in the kitchen with the nurse and she's drinking
tea. She's listening to the wireless, smoking her fag and paying
me no heed. I tell her I was expecting a card from my sister
and that it never came. She says that there's lots of cards
posted out at this time of the year and sometimes they come
late because of the amount of cards the postman has to hand
out. She says that maybe with the distance that card has to
travel between my sister and me it might be after Christmas
before I get it. She says to wait and see. There's not much
crack after that so I wander off.

I go to Kellie Castle and spend the morning there. Nobody

bothers you here and you can go about the place and do what you like. The man that has the place is a good enough man and he's always chipping away at stones and making some kind of statues with them and he never bothers if I sit about the place and watch him working. If you hang about long enough you'll get juice and a biscuit when the woman brings a drop tea to the man and when he takes his break he'll sit down and crack to you for a while before he starts chipping away at the stones again.

In the afternoon I'm up at the Gillingshill reservoir and by the time I'm over the fields and back to Ovenstone it's nearly dark. There's a man leaning on a shiny red car at the front of the building and he's got a big smile on his face and looks pleased with himself. He has two wee lassies with him and he says to me, 'This is Edna and Ethel.' I look at them and one's fine and the other one's glaickit. I pay them no heed and start up the stone steps just as the matron's coming out the building. She says they're all going to a Christmas party down in Anstruther and asks me if I'd like to come too and I say no. I'm still too upset not to have heard from Maggie.

It's sandwiches for tea because the cook's away and it's just me and a nurse that needs feeding. The nurse says that the two wee lassies looked very pretty in their party dresses and that I should have gone with them to the Christmas party in Anstruther. She says that Santa Claus would be at that party and if I'd gone with them I would have got a present from him.

When I'm finished with the sandwiches I say that I'm going for a wander and she tells me not to go far. She says that if she shouts for me then I've to come straight back and that she doesn't want to be hunting about in the dark for me. I tell her that I'll be back when she shouts and she's fine with that.

The snow stops as quick as it starts and there's nothing lying on the ground. The matron said that we might be in for a white Christmas and if we are then it will have to do better than this. I wander down the road and can see all the Christmas lights in the wee cottar houses and they look warm and cosy. I'm up the side of the field and the sheep look to see what I'm up to and when I pay them no heed they go back to grazing. At the old wooden gate I can hear Sandy and Peggy cracking in their tent a short distance away. It's not a real tent they have, not like the tents you would get from a camping shop – this is one that they've made themselves. It's a bit of green canvas stretched over sticks that are fastened in the ground and on top of the canvas you have bits of old carpets and bits of old rugs and anything else that would keep the wind and sleet out. They whole thing's weighed down with big stones and that camp would stay where it is supposing you had a howling gale raging. I'm leaning on the gate when the old man comes out.

'Oh it's you,' he says.

'Aye, it's me.'

'I heard you coming,' he says and he must have ears like a dog because I'm quieter than a mouse when I go about this place. He's over to the gate, him at the one side and me at the other and I look at him and he looks at me. 'Where's the other lads?' he says, and I tell him they're away home to their own people for Christmas and that I'm left in the place myself now. She comes from the tent and she's pleased to see me too. She's smiling and has a cheery look about her. She says she's glad that I've come back to see them again and that she knew I would be back. There's a nip in the air and she says we'd be better cracking in the tent where it's warmer. I go in the tent with them and it's a different world inside this camp.

A fire burns in an old drum that sits on three flat stones in the middle and a funnel takes the reek out the drum and then out the tent so they're not smoked out the place. Sandy sits cross-legged and tells me to sit too. On top of the drum you have an old pot lid and he lifts that to throw a few sticks on the fire and the drum's red-hot and the funnel's red hot too. Even with the heat in this camp Peggy's old coat is pulled tight about her and I think she would keep that coat on supposing the sun was splitting the pavements. This tent is warmer than any of the rooms you would get in the children's homes where it's just the bare pipes you have to keep you warm and half the time they're stone cold. I look at Sandy and I wonder how he manages to keep the two shoes on his feet because there's no toes or laces in them. A wee candle flickers and that's all there is to light up their faces along with the fire glow. He's friendly and she's friendly and I'm fine sitting in this tent with them.

Sandy asks if I see much of my sister and I tell him that I don't. I tell him that the Welfare moved her to Aberdeen and I don't think I'll be seeing much of her at all now and he says that's a shame. It's a while since he was in Aberdeen he says, but if he's ever back up that way he'll have a good look round the place and see if he can maybe catch Maggie and see her for a wee while. He says that my mother was never done looking for me and my sister and that if she'd got us then we would have been finished with the children's homes and we would all have been a family again. He tells me I've got a dose of brothers and sisters and he asks if the Welfare had held that back from me.

Peggy says, 'I went round all the children's homes with your Mammy trying to find you and your sister but we never got you Sandy. If you were in one place and they knew we were onto you they would get us shifted and they would have us shifted out the whole town to keep us from you seeing you. Do you remember the old woman that went about on the two sticks in Leven?'

'Aye.'

'Sadie was her name and you got the shops for her.'

'Aye.'

170

'Well your mammy got that woman and here's what she gave to your mammy.' She's raking about in an old bag now and it's a folded bit of paper she comes out with. She holds it next to the candle and squints her eyes to look at it, and it's a wee picture she has. 'That's what Sadie gave to your mammy. It's a wee picture that you made at the school. Can you remember drawing that picture Sandy?'

'No.'

'Well, you drew it and your mammy kept that wee picture for long enough and I keep the wee picture now.'

She tells me that my Mammy would never part with that wee picture because that was all she had that belonged me and she had no photos or anything else to remind her of me and that's why she liked the picture. She would look at that picture for a while, sometimes for about an hour, and if you said to her, 'What are you looking at Mary?' she would say, 'A wee picture that my laddie drew at the school.'

'If she's still looking for me you can tell her where I am now.'

'She can't look for you now Sandy!'

'How no?'

She looks at him and he looks at her. 'I don't think the laddie knows,' she says.

'You'll have to tell him,' he says.

She leans forward and says to me. 'Your mammy's dead now Sandy.'

'Aye.'

'Did you know that?'

'No.'

'She's been dead a while now.'

'Aye.'

'Are you alright?' she asks.

'Aye. I'm fine.'

She says the Welfare should have told me that my mother

had died and that they probably left it out because they didn't want to upset me and I told her that the Welfare never bothered about upsetting bairns and maybe they just forgot to tell me. Sandy says that the Welfare would know fine that my mammy was dead because there's nothing they don't know about folk. He says they know more about what's happening with people than the people know themselves. 'Supposing you do something and you think that nobody knows about it then you can guarantee that the Welfare would know about it,' he says.

I sit a good while in the tent with them. Peggy puts a pot on the fire to boil some water and makes a drop tea. She hands me mine in a bean tin and says to watch because the tin will be hot. It's an old chipped china mug that Peggy takes her tea in and when Sandy wants to drink he just lifts the kettle and takes it straight from the spout and she says nothing to him about that.

I'm looking at his pipes and it's a good set of bagpipes that he has there. I ask if he can get a tune out of them and he says that he can. I ask him to give them a blow and he says he'll not be playing them tonight because it's too late now. 'People would be putting the police onto me for playing them at this time of night,' he says.

He says if I listen out in the morning he'll play his pipes for me and I'll be able to hear them in Ovenstone. You can hear the pipes for miles he says and he asks me what tune I'd like him to play. I say I'm fine with any tune and he says that he'll pick a good one for me and tells me to listen out for the pipes in the morning.

I'm weary and Peggy says it's about time I was getting back to Ovenstone. Old Sandy says he'll walk me back to the place and Peggy's out the tent to see me off when I leave.

My Uncle Sandy leaves me at the fort and I'm halfway over the grass when I see a car coming in the place. It's a police car and a sergeant gets out. He tells the matron to make sure that all the doors are locked and that all the windows are fastened because he's got word that there's tinks going about and you've to watch that they don't break into the place and steal everything. The matron says that she'll make sure the building's secure before she goes to bed. The policeman says he's going to warn everyone else in the area about the tinks now.

'The tinks won't break into the place,' I say.

'Yes they would!' he says.

'No they wouldn't!'

'And how would you know?'

'Because I was speaking to them.'

'You were speaking to them?'

'Aye.'

'When were you speaking to them?'

'A wee while ago. I've been sitting in their camp with them. My Uncle Sandy walked me back to this place.'

'What do you mean your Uncle Sandy walked you back to this place?' the matron asks.

'They told me they were my Auntie and Uncle. I was in their tent in the woods and I was speaking to them.'

'The tinks!'

'Aye.'

'You'll have to put a stop to this,' she says to the sergeant. 'He shouldn't be mixing with the tinks,' he says.

I'm out the bath and in my pyjamas when the matron comes to see me. She goes on about the tinks and says that I've to stay away from them because they will get me in trouble. If anything goes missing about here it will be the tinks to blame she says and they're never done getting into trouble and keeping a carry-on that lot. I tell her that I like my Auntie and Uncle and that my Uncle says he'll play a tune on his pipes for me tomorrow and he says I've to listen out for it. She says that they might not even be there in the morning because they move about a lot and never stay for long in the one place and that even if they say they will be here tomorrow they might not be. I get into bed and the matron and a nurse sit with me for a bit. Tomorrow will be Christmas Eve and if I want lots of presents for Christmas then they say I'll need to stay away from the tinks and behave myself. I ask the matron if she knows that I have a dose of brothers and sisters and she says that she doesn't know anything about that and that I would need to ask the Welfare about that sort of thing. She tells me to get a good night's sleep because tomorrow will be a busy day for me and that we'll need to look for a good sock to hang up for Santa to fill with sweets and stuff for me.

'Do you know anything about my mammy?' I ask.

'No,' she says.

'I do.'

'What do you know about your mammy Sandy?'

'She's dead.'

The matron doesn't say anything except to go to sleep.

The next day I'm up early and I shouldn't have bothered because they keep a grip of me and don't let me out the place. I'm bored out my skull and I'm raging because I never heard Sandy playing his bagpipes. The matron tells me she was on the phone to Dr Carlyle and he says that I've to get extra medication with all the excitement with the tinks and I get twice the dose I would normally get and that just makes me tired and not fit to do anything. I fall asleep in a chair and when I wake nobody's about so I'm out the place quick.

I'm straight up to the camp and standing looking at things and there's bugger all to see bar an old metal pot and a few rusted cans. Sandy and Peggy have buggered off and if it wasn't for the ashes on the ground you would never know that anyone had even been here. I wonder where they've shifted to and why they've shifted without telling me they were leaving.

Maybe the matron was right about them when she said that they never stay long in a place and just bugger off when they feel like it. Maybe they shifted to another wood. I jump the fence and make my way to the farm at the top of the road where I meet a man with a wooden leg. I've seen this man before and he's fine with me. 'Do you know where the tinks have gone?' I ask him.

'The police put them out the wood last night,' he says.

'What for?'

'Because they're not supposed to be camping in that wood.'

'That was my Auntie and Uncle in that camp.'

'Was it?'

'Aye, do you know where they went?'

'They'll be away back to where they came from.'

'Where's that?'

'I don't know,' he says.

I look everywhere for them. I look in every wood I know and anywhere else I can think that they might put up a camp. I ask a dose of people if they've seen them, but no one seems to know where they've gone and the only thing I can do now is ask the matron to phone the police and ask where they put them. She tells me the police shifted them because they were being a nuisance in the area and that I should forget all about them now that they're away and not likely to be back again. I tell her that I liked seeing them in the wood and that I want to visit them again and that I would like to get to know them better. She's fed up with me going on about my Uncle and Auntie and goes away. I sit on the stone step and I'm still sitting there when the nurse calls me for my tea. When I'm finished my grub I see the nurse's fags and matches sitting on the table. I open the matchbox and put a few matches in my pocket. Then I go to the woods.

I'm standing where the camp was and there's bugger all to see. Sandy and Peggy are gone now and there's nothing left in this wood but the memory of them. I liked hearing their crack. I liked Peggy's cheery ways and Sandy's genuine friendliness towards me. I was pleased that they were my Auntie and Uncle, it meant something to me. They were a part of me, just like Maggie is a part of me, and they were the best people that I had met in my life. They told me that I had other brothers and sisters and they told me that I had more Aunties and Uncles. The Welfare must know these things. Why do they not tell me about my family? Why do they want to keep me away from them? What did my mother do that was so wrong that I had to be taken away from her? Why was I never allowed to see her again? I needed answers. I'm standing at the gate, looking at this wood, and my mind's racing. The Welfare have moved my sister far away from me. The police have moved my Uncle and Auntie from this wood, and my mammy is dead. I go where it's dense and thick with trees and put a match to them. Then I bugger off across the fields.

A week or so later, Rabbit's back in the place and I'm sitting with him and Tommy on the stone steps. I tell them that the tinks in the wood were my auntie and uncle and that I put a match to the trees on Christmas Eve.

'You only burnt a bit of the wood,' Tommy says.

'Aye, but it was a good bit,' I say.

'Were the fire engines at it?' Rabbit asks.

'Aye, and if they hadn't been that wood would have been burnt to a crisp and there wouldn't be a stick left in the place!'

Tommy never bothered to ask me why I put a match to the wood but Rabbit did and I told him it was because my aunt and uncle were shifted and because my mammy was dead. He told me his mammy was still living and he was fine with that but wished his father was dead. He says he doesn't want to go back home ever again and that next Christmas he wants to stay in this place with me.

When the lessons start again, Mr Watson picks four bairns out to go swimming at the Waid Academy school in Anstruther. I'm picked and pile into his van with Tommy and two other lads. It's a wee mini van that Mr Watson has and it's me that sits in the front with him and the other three lads sit in the back. When you come into Pitenweem you have a hump on the road and he puts his foot down and picks up speed before flying over that hump like a racing driver. The wheels of the van leave the road completely and you're flying through the air like an aeroplane. And what a thump you get when the wheels land at the other side. There's a dose of bairns in this Waid Academy school and they come from all the villages and farms round about and you get them all ages and when you look at them they all look the same dressed in their school uniforms. Us lads just wear what we like because we're not here for lessons and you don't need a uniform to swim in the school pool. You get about an hour at the swimming and you can roar and splash about while Mr Watson keeps an eye on you. When we're back to the place he tells us the swimming will be a regular thing once a week and that he'll only be picking out lads that have behaved themselves all week. So if you want to go swimming at the Waid Academy, you can't keep a carry-on in the place.

One day we're going through the woods and we find a dead fox. Tommy gets it by the tail and swings it round his head and whacks its ribs off a tree. He drags it back to the place by the tail and we get a bit string round its neck and hang it from a branch. We have big sticks and we're whacking this dead fox with them and when we're fed up with that we gather stones and throw them at the thing and the nurses pay no heed to what we're doing. When we're bored with this we bugger off and it's left dangling with Tommy's stick rammed up its arse.

When we got a living creature we were a bit more careful about things and one day we came across a kestrel that couldn't fly. Tommy said we should kill the thing to put it out its misery but the rest of us wanted to keep it living so we carried it back to the place and got our teacher Miss Kelly to have a look at it. She said its wing was broken and it would need to be fixed by a vet. That vet had that bird for four days before we got it back from him and Miss Kelly said we were going to look after it and nurse the thing back to health. She brought in a book that had everything you needed to know about birds in it and we found out what that bird liked to eat and where it builds its nest, how many eggs that bird would lay and other stuff like that. She told us it was a lassie bird and that we did the right thing when we rescued it because it was sore needing the attention of a vet. We kept it in a cage at the back of the classroom and the teachers took photographs of us holding it and pinned them on the walls. And we had a dose of pictures by the time that bird was fixed and ready to be set free. The day came to let it go and the teachers took it outside and opened the cage but the thing wouldn't come out and just sat there looking at us. Miss Brown told us to stand back and to ignore the bird and when we did that it came out and stretched its wings. It started to hop about a bit and you could see it looking up at the sky and you knew it was thinking about flying away. When it decided to go it just flew round the place a couple of times before landing back at the cage. 'Don't go near it,' she says, because she thinks it will fly off again. And it did. This time it went for good and that was the last we saw of it.

One day Miss Black came and said that she was going to visit Maggie and that if I wanted her to know anything she would pass a message on for me. She said Aberdeen was very far away and that it would take a whole day to get there by car and that she didn't have time to take me because she was responsible for a dose of bairns and every single one of them wanted something from her. The matron in Ovenstone said that it would be nice to see my sister more often but that it was down to the Welfare to sort that out for me. But, Miss Black never heeded what you wanted. I just got more fed up with things and I never bothered about behaving myself and just got worse and worse. I just wished they'd take me to see her but they wouldn't. I felt very alone in the world.

Dr Graham wasn't a real doctor and was just learning to be one. One day he asks me if I'd like to go out for a drive with him. I get in the car and he drives down to Pittenweem and we go to the beach. I know the best bits to walk along this shore and I show the man how to catch crabs and other stuff that goes about beaches and rock pools. He has his socks off and the trousers are pulled up to his knees and he's having a rare time at the seaside. The sun's shining and we're a while on this beach and he talks about lots of different things to me and I'm fine with the man.

After a while he starts to ask about places I was in before I came to Ovenstone and it's not just the homes he wants to know about, but the foster families I was with too. He wants to know what went on in the places, what happened to me and my sister and whether we liked the people or not. I get fed up with him and tell him to shut his pus because I don't like to talk about those things. When he keeps up with the questions about my past I run away from him and make my way up the path to the top of the cliffs. He shouts for me to stop but I pay him no heed and keep going. By the time he's up the path I'm sitting on the grass and he comes and sits with me and this gets me raging again. I get to my feet cursing and go to the cliff edge. He tells me to come back from the edge because he's worried that I might fall over. I ignore him and he comes towards me. I've never been raging like this in my life before and I lift a really big stone and scream at him to stay away from me or I'll fucking smack him with it. But he's worried about my safety and just keeps coming so I launch the stone with both hands and it smashes into his kneecap. He hits the deck and I can see that his leg's in a bad way. I storm off and make my own way back to Ovenstone and I never saw that man again. When I've calmed down I'm sorry about what's happened but he was the doctor and should have known when to stop pushing so hard. Talking about things only makes me angry. I've told them why hundreds and hundreds of times but they never listen.

Other times when you went to the beach it was the nurses that went along with you and they never bothered with questions about your past and they just let you bugger about and do what you liked while they sunbathed. Elie had a good beach with plenty of sand to run about on and you had rock pools to look for crabs in, but the best thing about this beach was the donkeys. If you got there early enough you never had to queue and you could get on a donkey straight away. The nurses are not sure about letting us on, but the man says they're canny enough beasts that are good with bairns and that reassures them.

'What's the fastest one?' I say to him.

'They all go the same speed,' he says.

I look at them and pick out the best beast and jump on its back. Rabbit's on one and Tommy's on one too and we're lined up and ready to start when this lassie comes over and takes a grip of my donkey.

'What are you doing?' I say.

'I'll be leading the donkey for you,' she says.

'Bugger off – I can ride the thing myself!'

The man steps in and says that the donkeys know to just walk along to a wooden post then turn round and walk back again and that we'll be fine. We plod off and it takes ages for these donkeys to get halfway to the post because they're lazy buggers and we're bored.

'Let's have a race,' Tommy whoops.

I dig my heels in and take a good grip of the reins and that gets the thing trotting. Rabbit's donkey keeps up with mine, but Tommy's beast just walks and that's got him raging. 'Will you fucking move!' he shouts, but the beast pays him no heed, so he's down on the sand to lift a good stick, then he's back on its back to give it a whack. That gets the thing moving and what a noise it makes as it flies past me kicking the sand up with its hooves and braying like a banshee.

'Get off that donkey!' the man roars as he runs along the beach, but there's no stopping that beast and it's round the wooden post at the speed of a racehorse and galloping back to the safety of the man and Tommy's still whacking its arse with the stick.

By the time we're dismounted, the man's raging and puts us off the beach.

'Don't bring them back to Elie because they're banned!' he shouts.

We pay him no heed and me, Tommy and Rabbit are over the rocks and on the lookout for anything that crawls or swims. We collect crabs in a pail to take back and show the nurses but Tommy just takes the shells off their backs and rips the arms and pincers off them before throwing them back in the sea and he never bothers to show the nurses anything he finds at the beach.

The nurses have their tops off when we get back to them, but you can't see anything because they're lying on their bellies. So we're down to the ocean to fill our pails and when we come back again we throw the cold water over their backs and that gets them up roaring at us and we gawk at their tits. The nurses keep us going in sandwiches and cups of juice and we spend hours at the seaside and it's about teatime when we pack up and go back to the place with our arms and backs burnt with the sun.

Having the nurses at the beach was good enough but what we never liked was when they decided to walk through the woods and the fields with us. They were no use at getting over fences or dykes and by the time they got a gate to let them through we were miles in front and you would be back in the place before you saw them again.

One day we're sitting on the grass verge when two laddies come walking up the road. We're up to them and asking who they are and what they're doing here.

'We're out for a walk,' the biggest lad says.

'Where are you from?' Tommy asks.

'St Andrews.'

'What are you doing at our bit?' I say.

'We're visiting our granny and just looking about.'

'You can't look about here,' Tommy says.

'How no?' asks the big lad.

'Because this is our place – now bugger off,' I say.

This lad's not scared of us and says he's done a bit of boxing before and I think he would set about us if we pushed him. He's a big lad and when you think about things maybe you're better not to tangle with the likes of him unless you have a big stick in your hand so we decide to pull back for now.

'If they go up that road then they've to come back down that road,' I say.

'Aye, and we'll be waiting for them,' adds Tommy.

The lads make their way up the hill and when they're out of sight we arm ourselves with good solid sticks and wait for them to come back again.

'That big lad's a boxer,' says Rabbit.

'Aye.'

'And for all we know he might be a prize fighter.'

'Are you faird?' Tommy asks him.

'Aye.'

'Well bugger off then,' I say.

'Aye bugger off!' Tommy says too.

Rabbit throws his stick over the fence and walks away. Tommy's right at the back of him and whacks him over the head with his stick and Rabbit gives out a yelp and falls to the ground with his hands on his head. I'm over quick to give Tommy four rapid whacks with my stick and that puts him in a daze. Next I land him a punch and that puts him on his arse and a kick in the pus has the blood pishing out his nose. He's roaring and that gets the attention of the nurses and it's Mr Watson that gets to us first. He tells me to put the stick down but I stand up to him and threaten to bash his brains out and before you can sneeze they have a grip of me and drag me up to the building. When they get me in the place they have me on the ground and three of them sit on me. One on my chest, one on my middle and one on my legs and when I calm down they just keep sitting on me for about an hour and never let me move a muscle and I can roar and curse as much as I like because they just sit there and pay no heed.

They increase my medication again. I have to take that because if I don't they won't let me out to run about. As long as you take your medication you can do what you like in this place and you're better to get it down your neck because that gets them off your back and you can get back to normal then. They plan more trips to Edinburgh for me because they want to do more tests. They want to find out what's causing my temper tantrums and why I'm so angry. They think there might be something abnormal about me and maybe my brain isn't working right. But the only thing that's wrong with my brain is the fact that it's fucked up. They've taken my parents from me. They've taken my sister from me, my aunt and uncle are gone. Every single person that means anything to me is quickly taken out of my life, and still they wonder why I'm angry.

I get a new man to see me and his name's Dr Sharpe and I don't think much of him. All that man does is look at you while he fiddles about with an orange and you hardly get a word from him. I just look at him too and he gets fed up with me doing that and tells me to bugger off.

I'm back playing with Tommy and me, him and Rabbit are just fine with each other again. One morning we have our lesson outside on the grass but in the afternoon it rains so Miss Kelly has us back in the classroom. Miss Shepherd is the one that's in charge and she's the one that keeps us right, but she's away today and we're left with Miss Kelly to teach us on her own.

The lesson starts good enough with a nature programme that comes off the wireless and when that's finished this woman starts going on about the whole thing again and tells us the same stuff that the woman on the wireless has already told us and I'm bored with it so I stand up.

'What are you doing Sandy?' she says.

'I'm going out.'

'You can't just leave the class,' she says.

I pay her no heed and make for the door, but she's quick and blocks my way and that gets me raging. She says I've to stay in the class and that she's not going to let me out and that just gets me wilder. I'm roaring at her now and when she still pays no heed I lift a chair. She just walks calmly away and sits down. She puts her hands on her thighs and looks straight in front of her and I'm over to her with this chair and ready to bring it down on her head. That woman never flinched and she never looked at me and she never said bugger all. I threaten to bring it crashing down on her skull but that makes no difference to her and she still keeps quiet and just sits as if nothing's happening. If she would say something or look at me then I could just whack her. But she does bugger all. I throw the chair across the room and it smashes off the wall and breaks in bits. Then I bugger off.

Miss Black visits and tells me that I'm getting too old for this place now. She says I need to be going to a proper school and mixing more with other bairns. And it's about time I was moving on. She says that they have found a nice children's home for me. She says that the man that runs this place is exceptionally good with young troubled boys and he'll be more useful and helpful to me than the staff in Ovenstone are. So there are no more tests in Edinburgh for now and no more Rabbit or Tommy. I think I'll miss them. Two weeks later I'm shipped out the place.

St Margaret's

I'm in the dining room, standing at the window, looking over the sand and sea. This is St Margaret's children's home in Elie and David Murphy (Uncle Dave) runs the place along with another woman who I've to call Aunt Margaret. I was told that I was in this home as a baby when I was first taken away from my parents. Aunt Margaret had looked after me and my sister then. But I had no memory of either the place, or Aunt Margaret, so as far as I was concerned this was just another move. Miss Black's told me that Uncle Dave's an ex-policeman and she's advised me not to keep a carry-on with this man because he knows how to handle lads that step out of line. He's a tall man and goes about in shorts that are a size too small for him and he's got them pulled tight up his arse. The hair's swept back on his head and it's tennis shoes that he wears on his feet and his socks are like the wee ankle socks I had to wear in Greenbanks.

I'm told to wait in the dining room while Miss Black chats to Uncle Dave in the office. When she comes out she says that she's going now and tells me to behave myself in this place and to do whatever Uncle Dave tells me to do. I follow her outside and when she drives off Uncle Dave has his arm round my shoulders like he's known me for a hundred years.

As soon as Miss Black's gone he has me back in the building and takes me upstairs to the bedroom to show me where I'll be sleeping. There are five beds in this room and the view from this window is even better than the view you had from the dining room downstairs.

He tells me to put on the new clothes that he's laid out for me. I start to undress and he stands watching me so I stop what I'm doing and look back at him and he leaves the room.

It's short trousers he has for me and they're too small so I leave them off and look out the window again. It's raining but there are people walking on the beach and I watch them. I can see the harbour and the lighthouse from here and I wonder if the donkey man's still going about, and if he is, I hope he's lifted my ban and lets me back on his donkeys and back on the beach now that I'm living in this place.

When I turn round Uncle Dave's standing in the doorway and he's looking at me again. He asks why I don't have my shorts on and I tell him that they're too small for me and he says to squeeze into them. I lift the shorts and he walks over to me and yanks my underpants to my ankles and tells me to put on the new pants that he's laid out for me. He watches me all the time and when I ask what he's looking at he takes a grip of me and gives me a smack on the bare arse with his hand and tells me not to be so cheeky then he leaves the room.

I go over to the dressing table and look in the mirror. I can see his handprint right across the cheeks of my arse and I wonder why the man did that to me. I put on the underpants and squeeze into the shorts, but the only way I can wear them is if I leave the top two buttons out and don't fasten them. When I'm dressed I look in the hall but nobody's about and the place is quiet. I go back to the window and watch the people going about on the beach.

He's back and tells me to come downstairs and sit in the dining room. He says the other bairns are still at school and that they'll be home in an hour and he tells me to sit and wait here for now.

I wonder what Rabbit and Tommy are doing. I wish I was back in Ovenstone where I would probably be running about in the woods or playing up at the reservoir and I would feel a lot better than I do in this place. Suddenly it dawns on me that I might never see Rabbit and Tommy again. I've been shifted so many times in the past and I've never missed anyone bar my sister, but I miss Tommy and Rabbit.

The dining tables are long and that tells me that there's a good dose of bairns in this place and I think there will be a lot more bairns here than there were in Ovenstone. We were all about same age in Ovenstone but Miss Black has told me that you get them all ages in this place and that there will be a lot of lads who are bigger and older than me in St Margaret's.

I'm in the hall when all the bairns come through the door and each boy holds out his fingers for Uncle Dave to smell. I'm wondering what this is all about and notice that he keeps a couple of the lads back. The rest of the boys go quietly to their rooms to change into their play clothes and Uncle Dave takes the two lads that he's kept back up to his own bedroom.

'What's up with them?' I ask a boy who's looking at me.

'They've been smoking,' he says.

'How does he know they've been smoking?'

'Because he can smell the smoke off their fingers.'

'What will happen to them?'

'They'll get the belt.'

'Will they?'

'Aye, and they'll get it on the bare arse.'

'The bare arse!'

'Aye, that's what you get if you're caught smoking.'

'The belt on the bare arse?'

'Aye. You get the belt for anything you do wrong in this place.'

'Have you had the belt?'

'Aye.'

'On the bare arse?'

'Aye.'

'How many times.'

'Loads of times,' he says.

The lassies don't have to hold their fingers out for Aunt Margaret to smell and she seems to be pleased to see the girls. She says hello to each lassie as they come in the door and she's fine with them and the lassies seem to be fine with her.

I can't make up my mind about St Margaret's. And I can't make up my mind about the man who's in charge either, and I'll just have to wait and see what goes on in this place before I decide.

At teatime I get my first good look at all the other bairns. The boys sit at Uncle Dave's table and the lassies sit with Aunt Margaret at the girls' table along with the younger bairns that are in the place. Before you get your grub Uncle Dave picks out a laddie to say a prayer and here's what the lad has to say:

> For what we are about to receive,
> May the Lord make us truly thankful,
> Amen.

After your tea you have prep. Prep is where you do any homework that the school has given you and if you've no homework to do then Uncle Dave gives you an essay or hands you a book to read.

'How long do we have to do this for?' I ask the boy next to me.

'For an hour,' he whispers.

'What are you whispering for?'

'Because if you're caught talking during prep you get the belt.'

It seems that if you do anything wrong in this place then it's the belt you get. I just sit quietly looking at the daft wee book that he's handed me and keep my mouth shut like the rest of them.

'You better learn what's in that book,' the lad says.

'How?'

'Because he'll ask you questions about it at the end of prep.'

'Will he?'

'Aye, to make sure that you've read it.'

Your bedtime goes by your age and for me it's set at eight o'clock. This place is nothing like Ovenstone where you could sit up late and watch a film if you liked and there's a lot more rules to follow in this place too.

I'm in bed and Uncle Dave comes in to say goodnight to the boys. He starts at one side of the room and moves from bed to bed giving all the lads a goodnight kiss. I'm the last one he comes to and he leans right over me and turns my head to face him then he plants his lips over my whole mouth and his mouth is soaking wet and I can feel his saliva all over my lips. I try to turn my head but he holds my face firmly with both hands and takes what seems like an age to finish kissing me.

'No talking,' he says, as he closes the bedroom door. And there's not a cheep from any of the other lads in the room. I'm left shocked and puzzled by this. None of my foster fathers had ever done anything like this before. Mr Watson in Ovenstone had never kissed me, so why has Uncle Dave? I rubbed my lips and could feel the wetness on the back of my hand – it was disgusting. It was my first night in this place and I took a long time to fall asleep.

The next day I'm waiting at the bus stop in my new school uniform with the rest of the bairns. It's a black blazer with red stripes round the edges and short grey trousers that I have on. Some of the lads are older than me and they look silly standing there with their long legs and short trousers. This is the first time I've had to wear anything like this in my life and I look and feel stupid.

The bus takes you through the villages of St Monance and Pittenweem to pick up more bairns on its way to the Waid Academy school in Anstruther. This is the same school that I went to from Ovenstone for the swimming and I never thought I'd see the day when I would be getting my lessons in this place.

The class I'm in has a dose of bairns in it and you only have one teacher to teach them all. A boy next to me says, 'Hey you, new boy, are you from the Elie home?'

'Aye, how do you know?'

'Because you have short trousers on. All the home boys wear short trousers.'

'Do they?'

'What are you in the home for?'

'Nothing.'

'You can't be in the home for nothing. You must have done something wrong. What did you do?'

I tell him to shut his pus and he doesn't like that and offers to fight me at playtime. I lean over and give him a punch in the lug and that's him roaring and me marched to the head-master's office. The headmaster thinks I'd be better in the dunces' class where they can keep a closer eye on me. That's where they put me next and I'm fine with that, because you only have about ten bairns in the dunces' class.

At playtime I'm outside and don't know anyone so I just wander about with my hands in my pockets. I can pick out other lads from the home easily enough because they stand out like sore thumbs in their short trousers. Some of these lads are about fourteen or fifteen and you can see that they're embarrassed and they just stand about waiting for the play-time to finish so they can get back to their lessons.

If you do anything wrong in the school the headmaster gets straight on the phone to the home about it and you have Uncle Dave to face when you get back to St Margaret's after school.

I'm standing outside Uncle Dave's bedroom along with a few other lads that have misbehaved and we've to wait ages for him to come and deal with us. One lad, smaller than me, is already in tears just thinking about what's to come, but the other lads say nothing and just wait for Uncle Dave to arrive. When he takes the first laddie in you can hear him yelping as he gets his punishment and when he comes out again the tears are rolling down his face and he's holding his arse and I can see the belt marks on his thighs below his shorts. The other laddies all get the same and then it's my turn.

'Come in the room,' he says. He looks at me and I look at him. I can see the leather strap stuck down the side of his shorts and sticking out at the top.

'You're no touching me with that!'

He tries to get a grip of me, but I wriggle free and bolt down the stairs. 'Come back here!' he roars, but I pay him no heed and run down the stairs and go through the front door and out the building.

I'm outside and some of the lads are playing football on the grass. I'm raging and go out the gate and that's me on the beach and out the grounds of the place. I look back and can see Uncle Dave watching me from his upstairs window.

I make my way along the beach and then through the streets of Elie. I decide that I'm going to walk all the way back to Ovenstone because I know how to get to the place and once I get there the nurses and the matron will be just fine with me. I'll tell them that I don't like living in St Margaret's and I'll ask if I can come back to live in Ovenstone. Miss Black, the Welfare woman, is the person I should be telling this to. But I have no idea how to get in touch with her. She doesn't visit me very often and it could be long enough before I see her again. With Miss Black it's 'out of sight, out of mind'. So, it will have to be the matron in Ovenstone that I complain to.

A blue van stops beside me and Uncle Dave leans out the window. 'Where are you going Sandy?' he says.

'Back to Ovenstone.'

'Back to Ovenstone?' He looks surprised.

'Aye!'

'Are you not going to give this place a chance?' he asks.

I look at him and he has a smile on his face and he seems to be a lot nicer with me now than he was earlier. 'Did you think I was going to give you the belt?'

'Aye.'

'I was just going to tell you off for punching that boy in the school.'

I say nothing and he opens the van door and tells me to get in. 'You've nothing to worry about Sandy. I'm not going to touch you,' he says.

Miss Black comes to the home the next day after school. I think Uncle Dave must have got in touch with her and told her about my attempt to return to Ovenstone. She says she's going to have a word with Uncle Dave in the office first and then she'll have a word with me. When I'm called for he tells her about me punching the lad in the school and he says that when he tried to discipline me I ran away. He thinks maybe it was a bad idea to take me off my medication so quickly and he thinks they should start me up on the pills again. She agrees with him and says she'll have a word with the doctor about how much medication I should get. All they do is talk to each other and every time I open my mouth Miss Black tells me not to be rude and to stop butting in when adults are talking. She says that she thinks I'm angry and throwing fits because Uncle Dave won't let me do what I like in this place and she says that it's a firm hand I need and that I'll just need to learn the hard way if I keep a carry-on. I'm fed up with her and I'm fed up with him and walk out the office. I'm standing behind the boat shed when she comes back to her car and she drives off without noticing me.

They have some strange rules in this place and one of them is that the older boys get to sit on the soft seats and the younger boys have to sit on the hard wooden chairs. You can be sitting watching television and minding your own business when some big laddie comes along and tells you to shift. Even if that lad's only a day older than you he can tell you to shift. That's the rules in this place.

If there's a good film on the television Uncle Dave watches it too. When he comes in the room he picks out some of his favourite boys to come and sit with him, and he'll have one, or maybe even two boys, sitting on his lap at the same time, while others sit at his feet. They get turns to sit on his knee and most lads seem to think that it's a great honour and a privilege to do this. Some boys even have a smug look about them when sitting on Uncle Dave's knee, and seem to think that other boys are jealous of their exalted positions. As far as I'm concerned they can sit on Uncle Dave's knee for as long as they like, because I certainly have no desire to do that.

At the weekend you could kick a ball about on the beach with some of the other lads that never get much to do in this place. Uncle Dave takes some of his 'Pet boys' out in his boat and teaches them how to sail and stuff like that. When they're finished with the boats the same lads would be away out into the countryside with Uncle Dave on the bicycles that he's bought for them. Meanwhile, the other lads would be left in the place to get on with things by themselves.

'Have you to be a certain time in this place before you get a bike?' I ask this lad.

'I've been in this place for years and I've not got a bike yet,' he says.

'How's that.'

'Because Uncle Dave doesn't like me.'

'What's your name?'

'Specky Boy.'

'Is that what they call you?'

'Aye.'

'What do they call you that for?'

'Because I wear glasses.'

I look at him and he's got plasters round his specs to keep them together and to stop them falling off his face and he looks a right poor crater.

One day I have a fight with one of the older boys and he kicks the crap out of me and I've got two black eyes, a burst lip and sore balls.

'I'll need to teach you to fight,' Uncle Dave says.

'Aye.'

'You can come along to my wrestling class,' he says.

I'm outside with Specky Boy and I tell him I'm going to Uncle Dave's wrestling class to toughen me up.

'Do you want to come?' I ask.

'You have to be invited first,' he says.

'I'm inviting you.'

'You can't just invite people.'

'How no?'

'It's only Uncle Dave that can invite you,' he says.

You get the wrestling lessons in Uncle Dave's private sitting room next to his bedroom and me and three other lads are stripped to the waist and standing in our shorts waiting for the lesson to start.

He picks two lads to put on an exhibition match and me and this other boy stand back to watch them wrestle. Uncle Dave referees the match and you can only win by pinning the other lad's shoulders to the floor for the count of three. These lads are evenly matched and nobody manages a pin and Uncle

Dave gets fed up with them and stops the match and declares it a draw.

Now it's my turn to wrestle and Uncle Dave brings the big bugger that kicked the shite out of me earlier on into the room.

'I'm no fighting him,' I say.

The lad gives me an evil look and Uncle Dave says not to worry because it's only a friendly bout and he'll be the referee to make sure that he fights fair.

'This will be a submission fight,' Uncle Dave says.

'What's that?' I ask.

The big lad sneers. 'If you submit you lose.'

I look at him and he's about fifteen and near twice the size of me. The minute the match starts he gets his arm round my neck and has me in a headlock and I can hardly breathe because he's choking the life out of me.

'Do you submit?' the lad says.

'Break the hold!' Uncle Dave shouts.

When he comes at me again he falls to his knees and takes the legs from under me and I land on my arse. He turns me over and sits on my back. Then he gets his hands under my chin and pulls my head back to stretch my neck.

'Submit,' he shouts.

The lad's trying to snap my neck and I'm just about to submit when Uncle Dave shouts. 'Break the hold!'

This lad throws me about and gets me in a few more holds and I can't do a thing with him because he's too big and strong for me. He gets me in a back hammer and he's about snapping my arm when Uncle Dave shouts, 'Break the hold.' Next he wraps his legs round my neck and starts to squeeze the breath out of me. The lad's roaring at me to submit and Uncle Dave's kneeling down at my face. I manage to turn my head a wee bit and that lets me sink my teeth into the lad. I fasten onto his thigh and bite as hard as I can. 'Stop biting!' Uncle Dave roars, but I pay him no heed and keep my mouth clamped on the lad's thigh and he's punching hell out my back and squealing like a pig. 'Will you stop biting!' Uncle Dave roars again and it takes him and a few other laddies to prize me off that boy.

I never got back to the wrestling after that and it didn't bother me because I never thought much of it anyway. In future I would be quite content to watch the wrestling on the television.

Me and Specky Boy become pals and I look out for him and he looks out for me.

One day I say, 'Do you know what to do if a big lad picks on you Specky Boy?'

'No,' he says.

'Do you want me to show you?'

'Aye.'

I fall to my knees quick and pull the legs from under him and he's on his arse.

'That's what you do! You pull the legs from under them and then you can tackle them when they're on the ground.'

I practise the move with him a couple of times and he gets the hang of it quick and puts me on my arse a few times too. Practising wrestling moves is thirsty work and when we're done with that we go for a drink of water and there's a big lad standing at the door.

'Where are you going?' he says.

'Inside,' Specky Boy answers.

'Nobody's to get in.'

'How no?'

'Because Uncle Dave says I've to guard the door and not let anyone in – that's how!'

'But we want a drink of water.'

'Tough – now fuck off!' He pushes Specky Boy and we walk away.

'Why did you let him push you like that?'

'What am I supposed to do with a laddie that size?' he says.

'I showed you what to do with big lads.'

'Aye.'

'Why did you not pull the legs from under him?'

'Because.'

'Because what?'

'It might not work with him.'

'Of course it will work. It works on every big lad. You just need to get them on their arse and then you can tackle them.'

'You do it.'

'Me?'

'Aye, you,' he says.

'What do you want me to do it for?'

'Because you can do it better than me Sandy.'

'But you need to learn how to do it too. Just do to him what you did to me on the beach and you'll be fine.'

'Do you think so?'

'Aye, you'll do it no bother. Go back to him and give it a try.'

'Will you come with me?'

'Aye, I'll come. Just go right up to him and tell him you're going for a drink of water whether he likes it or not and if he tries to stop you, take the legs from under him and put him on his arse!'

'What do you want this time?' the big lad says.

'A drink of water.'

'Bugger off!'

He looks at me and when I give him the nod he drops to his knees and the big lad kicks him in the pus and smashes his specks. Looks like we'll need to work on that move a bit more.

As time goes on some of the bigger boys move out and other lads start to take their places as Uncle Dave's favourite boys.

I'm a year in the place now and he's showing more interest in me. I'm still wary of the place but it looks like I'm going to be stuck here for a while so I'm trying to make the best of it.

One day Uncle Dave's fixing the chain on a bicycle and shouts me over:

'Would you like to try a bike Sandy?'

'Aye.'

'Can you ride a bike?'

'Aye.'

'Let me see you ride this one then.'

I jump on the bike and pedal it up the path and round the whole building.

'You can ride that no bother,' he says.

'Aye.'

'I'll need to teach you how to ride a bicycle on the road now,' he says.

We pedal through the streets of Elie – me, two other lads and Uncle Dave. We cycle out to the country and I'm doing just fine until we come to a big hill. It's a steep hill and I'm pedalling like mad to keep up with the other two lads but run out of puff. I'm just about to get off the bike and push it when Uncle Dave comes alongside me. 'You're struggling a bit on this hill,' he says, and puts his hand on my arse to push me along. Every hill you come to he's got his hand on my arse and that man knows about every hill in Fife. I wish he wouldn't do it but as soon as I get better at going up hills he won't need to. And it's good to be out of the place and in the countryside on the bike.

Soon he's asking me if I'd like to try my hand at sailing. He says that before you can sail a yacht you have to learn to row a punt. I'm in my swimming trunks and so is he as he rows the boat. After a while he stops.

'What have you stopped for?'

'This is as far as we go,' he says.

'Do we go back in now?'

'Before I teach you to sail I need to make sure that you're a good enough swimmer.'

'I am.'

'Well let's see you swim back to the beach,' he says.

I look at the distance. 'The shore! That's miles away.'

'If you're out in a boat and anything goes wrong in that boat and it starts to sink then you have to be able to swim back to the beach,' he says.

I jump overboard and start to swim for the shore and that man rows the punt at the back of me to keep an eye on me. I come to a bit that's thick with seaweed and what a job I have to swim through that stuff and he says to stick at it or I'll be no use as a sailor. By the time I get to the shore I'm worn out, gasping for breath and half drowned.

I'm invited to his private lounge more often now, along with a few other boys. We get to watch late films on the television when the other boys are in their beds sleeping and you get biscuits and plenty of juice to drink.

When it's dark, the rats come out and you get them at the bins and the bike shed. Uncle Dave has a rifle and he lets the lads take shots at the rats and he asks me if I'd like to have a go. He shows me how to load the slug and when I see a rat I aim and pull the trigger. I manage to hit one and he says I'm a good shot and that he's thinking about taking me along to the rifle club in Pittenweem.

We're off school for the summer and Uncle Dave's thinking about which lads he's going to take on holiday with him to Butlins and I'm hoping that I get to go. Some of the older boys have already been told that they're going but the rest of us will just have to wait and see if we're picked or not. The week before the holiday he comes into my bedroom and wakens me from my sleep. He tells me to keep quiet and to come with him.

He takes me to his lounge and tells me to sit on a chair and watch the television. He goes to make a sandwich and when he comes back he has biscuits and juice for me. When I'm finished with that he tells me to come and sit on his knee. I'm not sure about doing this, but, to be honest, I'm quite happy to be up here in his room watching television and getting juice and biscuits and stuff like that while the other lads are lying in their beds. In a way I felt quite special, and I was pleased that he was beginning to take an interest in me and offering me more and exciting things to do. I also knew that he hadn't quite made up his mind about which lads he was taking with him to Butlins, and I certainly wanted to go on that holiday. I go and sit on his knee.

'Have you decided which lads you're taking with you to Butlins yet?' I ask.

'I'm still thinking about that,' he says.

'Will I be going?' I turn my head to look at him.

'Well that depends.'

'On what?'

'On how you behave between now and next week.'

'I've been behaving. I've hardly kept a carry-on in this place for ages.'

He strokes my hair and then my neck and I don't like that and move his hand away.

'Do you know what you get at Butlins Sandy?'

'Aye, a holiday.'

'Have you been on holiday before?

'Aye, I was in a caravan at St Andrews when I was in Greenbanks.'

'Butlins is a lot better than St Andrews.'

'You had the seaside at St Andrews,' I say.

'You have the seaside at Butlins,' he says.

'What else do you have at Butlins Uncle Dave?'

He tells me that you have a fairground and that all the rides are free and that you can go on them as many times as you like. You can stay on a ride until you're sick he says. Butlins has a picture house and a concert hall and you can see big stars singing and telling jokes all night. You can go swimming outdoors or indoors and you have snooker, table tennis and go-karts. You can do just about everything you ever wanted to do at Butlins.

'Will you take me – please?'

'I'll think about it,' he says.

He kisses the top of my head. He has one hand round my waist and strokes my face and neck with the other. He works his hand slowly downwards and toys with the elasticated waist of my pyjama bottoms. I tense and he says not to worry about anything. He tells me that he cares very much for me and would not do anything in the world to hurt me. His voice is gentle, soft, and soothing. His hand slips inside my pyjama bottoms and I instinctively thrust my hand down to stop him. 'You're not touching me there!' I say. This seems to have the desired effect and he stops what he's doing. He does not force the issue, lifts me off his knee, and gets to his feet. At first I think he is angry with me, but, when he puts his arm round my shoulders, I can see that he's more irritated than angry. We go back up the stairs and I note that he's careful to avoid every step that creaks, and I do the same. I get quickly into my bed and pull the blankets up to my chin. He kisses me gently on the forehead then creeps across the room and wakes another lad from his sleep. I watch in the semi darkness as he carries this boy out the room in his arms. Strangely, I have no sympathy for this lad and I am much more concerned with the fact that I may have lost my chance of a holiday to Butlins.

A day or two later, somebody breaks the conservatory window with a football and Uncle Dave's raging and says he's going to punish every boy in the place. He takes us all inside and up the stairs to the very top of the building. We're standing in a corridor and I've never been in this part of the building before, but some of the lads have and they tell me that this is Aunt Margaret's bedroom. All the boys are worried and one wee lad is already in tears at the thought of what's to come.

'What's wrong with you?' I say and one of the big lads tells me that he's had a few hidings from Uncle Dave before and that he's shitting himself.

Uncle Dave says he's going to give all the younger laddies a good hard spanking on the bare arse and that the older laddies will be getting the strap on the bare arse. He picks the boy that's crying to go first and the wee lad's terrified and frozen with fear. Uncle Dave takes a grip of his collar and marches him into the room. We can all hear the wee lad howling as Uncle Dave gives him a good bare arse spanking that seems to go on forever. When he comes out the lad's sobbing his heart out and the next boy's taken in. When it's my turn I'm not happy about things. I can see the leather strap stuck down the side of his shorts and I say, 'You're no touching me with that!' and he says not to worry because it's only the older lads who'll be getting the strap. I stand looking at him and he says that he knows it wasn't me that broke the window and that he's going to be lenient with me. He tells me to take my shorts and pants down and to lie across his knee. When I pay him no heed he says, 'Do you want to go to Butlins or not?' If I keep a carry-on I won't get the holiday to Butlins so I do what he wants. He wallops my arse and I just lie there and don't make a sound and if there was no Butlins to think about I would have broken every window in that building after he'd finished with me.

He finally tells us which boys will be going to Butlins and I'm one of the lads picked.

'I knew I wouldn't get to go,' Specky Boy says.

'I was just lucky to get picked,' I say.

'No, Uncle Dave likes you.'

'He likes you too.'

'Nobody likes me,' he says.

Butlins turns out to be everything Uncle Dave had said it would be – and more! It was a fantastic place to be with hundreds of carnival rides and amusements and the place was right next to the seaside – just like St Margaret's. It was a long journey down to Ayrshire, and Uncle Dave, being a slow and careful driver, had taken the best part of the day to get there. In the van I had thought about my friend Specky Boy and was sad that he had not been allowed to come on holiday with us. But, within five minutes of landing in that holiday camp I had forgotten all about him and I was whizzing about the place like a blue-arsed fly. Uncle Dave had forgotten to pack my medication and I was as high as a kite!

We had three chalets between us and I shared one with four other lads. Uncle Dave had relaxed the rules a bit while we were on holiday and he never bothered if we yapped in our beds at night. I must have kept the other lads up half the night ranting on about all the plans I had for the following day. There was just so much to do in this place that you never had time to get bored. The go-karts were about the only thing you had to pay to get on and Uncle Dave paid five times for me to get on the karts in one morning before putting his foot down and saying, 'Away and have a shot on something that's free!'

You never want a good holiday to end, but I just couldn't wait for the last day of this holiday. This was the day that I had looked forward to the most. This, for me, was the main event – we were going to the wrestling! They never told you who would be topping the bill in case the wrestler never turned up and your head was spinning trying to think who it would be. A whole dose of names flashed through my mind. Names like Mick McManus, Jackie Pallo, Les Kellet and others flooded my brain. First up you had some bugger that I'd never heard of before. To look at, you wouldn't think this lad was much of a wrestler at all. I paid him no heed, and waited to see who he was to fight and I just about wet myself when the ring master announced that his opponent was Kendo Nagasaki, complete with his trademark full face mask! They said that Nagasaki's trainer had not turned up and they asked for a volunteer to take his place. Uncle Dave was out his seat and in that ring before you could blink and his hands were all over Nagasaki's body to loosen him up for the match. I had my doubts about Nagasaki the minute he stepped in the ring. I had seen every single wrestler on the television, and this bugger seemed to have nothing like the build that the real Nagasaki had. I was convinced that the man behind the mask was a fake. At the end of round one I left my seat and made my way to Nagasaki's corner. Uncle Dave was patting him down and I asked him to pull the mask off Nagasaki's face to prove that he was a fake. But he just told me to shut up and to go and sit on my arse. Nagasaki won the fight but I booed him as he left the ring and hoped that whoever was starring in the main bout would be the real thing.

'Ladies and gentlemen, boys and girls, he's travelled thousands and thousands of miles, all the way from the dark African Jungle to this wrestling ring, right here, in the super Butlins holiday camp. Please put your hands together for the evil, devil witch doctor – Masambula!'

This was more like it. Everyone booed but I was ecstatic. Masambula came in the ring wearing a full-length leopard skin and the ringmaster assured everyone that Masambula had killed this dangerous African leopard with his own bare hands. When I looked at the wrestler who was to fight him I could see him shaking in his boots, and when Masambula rolled his eyes, I knew that this lad was for the pot!

It was a fantastic holiday. Uncle Dave was absolutely brilliant with me, and as far as I knew, he was brilliant with the other lads too. He really went out of his way to make sure that we all had a great time. Nothing was too much trouble for him. I had bonded really well with him and liked him a lot. He was the perfect father figure and I had almost forgotten that there was a darker, more sinister side to his nature. But all good things come to an end.

Back in St Margaret's I start to get more goes on the bike. Uncle Dave takes me and some other lads bicycle runs along the coast and you can cycle all the way to Anstruther and maybe even as far as Crail some days. The bike I have is not much to look at and you have no gears on it so your legs are scunnered when you're trying to make it up a hill on that thing. One night he comes for me when the other lads are sleeping and takes me from my bed. I'm sitting in his lounge and he says that he's been thinking about getting me a bigger and better bike.

'When?'

'Soon.'

'How soon?'

'That depends.'

'On what?'

He gets up and walks through to his bedroom and I follow.

'When will you be getting me a better bike?'

He sits on the edge of the bed. 'I was thinking about getting you one tomorrow.'

'Tomorrow!'

'Yes.'

'A new bike?'

'Yes.'

'Brand new?'

'Yes.'

'A racer?'

'Do you want a racer?'

'Aye.'

He starts to undress and takes everything off including his underpants. He gets into his bed with bugger all on.

'Do you not wear pyjamas?' I ask.

'No.'

'How no?'

'Because this room's too hot for pyjamas,' he says.

He pulls the blankets down at the side and tells me to jump in. He says I can lie in with him for a while and we can talk about what kind of bike he's going to get me. I tell him I want a racer with as many gears as you can get on the thing and he says if that's what I want then that's what I'll get. I go on about the bike for ages and when I get tired he says to just lie with him and he'll waken me early in the morning and I can go back to my room before the other lads are up.

'Jump in,' he says, patting the matress.

'Will I definitely get a racer bike?'

'Yes,' he says.

'Promise?'

'I promise.'

I get in his bed and he rolls on to his back and tells me to lie on top of him. I'm hesitant. It's not like the last time when I was just sitting on his knee. This time I'm in his bed and that makes me feel a lot more vulnerable. If he takes a grip of me there's not much that I can do to stop him because he's much bigger and stronger than me. But I have my heart set on that racer bike. He's back to his gentle manner now and trying his best to reassure me that I will be fine, and that he will not hurt me. He puts his arms round me and rolls me on top of him and rests my cheek on his chest. 'What are you going to do? I ask.

'Just relax – you'll be fine Sandy.' He slips both hands under my pyjama top and strokes my back. He is very gentle and trails his fingers down my spine.

'Will I definitely be getting my bike?'

'Yes.'

'Tomorrow?'

'Yes.' He starts to lower my pyjama bottoms. 'Lift your bum,' he says.

'Will I get my bike in the morning or the afternoon?' I ask, lifting my bum.

'Afternoon.' He slides my bottoms to my knees.

'And will it have racing handlebars?'

'Yes.' His hands are roaming over my arse now.

'And it will have a dose of gears on it?'

'Yes.' He rolls me onto my back and starts to play with me.

'And it will be my bike?'

'Yes.' He starts to play with himself now.

'And I won't have to share it with anyone else?'

'No.' His face starts to change.

'Promise?'

'Yesssss.' His face goes bright red.

'I better get the bike.'

'You will.' His face is contorted now.

'I fucking better get it!'

'You will!' He makes a mess all over me.

The next day I get my new bike and what a bike it is. A Falcon was the best bike you could get and it had racing handlebars and a dose of gears on it and the other lads were all jealous. Uncle Dave said I was to look after it properly and I wasn't to let anyone have a shot on it – and I didn't!

I'm allowed to go cycle runs on my own now and when I'm fed up in the place I just bugger off on my bike and cycle round the countryside. He's started to do more things with me now and he takes me to the swimming baths in Kirkcaldy, the picture house in Methil and when he buys a house for himself in St Monance he takes me there too. He has lots of repairs to do at his new house and he has other lads staying for weekends to help him out with the work. I get a lot more to do and have a lot more freedom than most of the lads in this place and one morning on the way back from swimming in Kirkcaldy I see my Uncle Sandy and Auntie Peggy. They're standing outside the post office in the main street of Lundin Links and I look from the van window, but they don't see me. I say nothing to Uncle Dave or any of the lads about them and just sit quiet in the van. When I'm back to the place I get on my bike and bugger off.

I go back to Lundin Links and cycle up and down every road and look in every bit wood, but I can't find them or the camp. I get fed up looking everywhere and decide to ask at a farm.

'What do you want?' the woman says.

'Do you know where the tinks are camped?'

'What do you want with the tinks?'

A man comes and stands with her. 'I'm trying to find my Uncle and Auntie.'

'What Uncle and Auntie?' the man asks.

'My Uncle Sandy and my Auntie Peggy.'

'Are they tinks?'

'Aye.'

'Where did you get that new bike?' the woman asks.

'From my Uncle.'

'What Uncle?'

'My Uncle Dave.'

'Is he a tink too?'

'No, he runs the home I'm in.'

'What home?'

'St Margaret's home in Elie.'

'Is that where you stay?'

'Aye.'

'Have you ran away from the place?'

'No.'

'I think we should get the police to this lad,' she says to him.

These people are no use to me so I bugger off. The next person I come across is an old man walking a dog.

'Do you know where the tinks are camped?'

'Is it old Sandy Stewart you're looking for?'

'Aye.'

'You'll get him in the wee wood next to the garage at Lundin Links.'

Sandy's snapping sticks when I arrive. 'Is that you?' he says.

'Aye it's me.'

'You're back to see us.'

'Aye.'

He wears a tartan bonnet and has a mottled neckerchief round his neck. He's got on two jackets, two pairs of trousers, a big overcoat and boots without laces. Wiping the sweat from his brow he says, 'I'm no sweating the day!'

I walk to the camp with him. 'God bless us,' she says when she sees me. Peggy puts her arms round me and I'm fine with that. She hands me tea in a jam jar and puts a piece in my hand with some kind of meat on it. They're pleased to see me and I'm pleased to see them.

Sandy tells me they were shifted from Ovenstone wood by the police and got a warning to stay away from me. She says it's as well they were shifted because some bugger put a match to the wood and they could have been burnt to a crisp if they'd still been camping there. She tells me that the Welfare goes all out to keep traveller bairns back from their families once they have a grip of them. But the bairns will always get back to their own people in time she says and she just wishes my mammy had been living to see me here now. I tell them I'm in St Margaret's home in Elie now and that my sister's still in Aberdeen.

'You miss Maggie, don't you?' she says.

'Aye.'

'Do you see much of her?'

'No.'

'Can you no ask the Welfare man to take you to see her?'

'It's a woman I've got.'

'Can you no ask her then?'

'She says she's too busy to be running up and down to Aberdeen with me.'

'Does she now?'

'Aye.'

'Is that what she says to you?'

'Aye.'

'Maggie will be left the school now.'

'Aye, the Welfare told me she's applying to be a nurse.'

'That's a good job to have,' Sandy says.

'Aye.'

'Would you like to see your father sometime?' she asks.

'Aye.'

'He's in a house now.'

'Aye.'

'You could maybe ask the Welfare woman to take you to see him.'

'Aye.'

'He's in Dundee, that's closer than Aberdeen.'

'Aye.'

'Maybe she'll have time to do that.'

'Aye.'

'Will you ask her to see him Sandy?'

'Aye.'

'It's your Auntie Mary he bides with. That's your father's sister and your brother Henry bides there as well.'

Sandy gives me my father's address and tells me to ask the Welfare about seeing him because he's not keeping well and it would be good for me to see him.

'Do you think he'll want to see me?' I ask her.

'Of course he'll want to see you Sandy.'

'I would rather see my Mammy.'

'I know you would son.'

When I'm back in the place I go looking for Uncle Dave. When I get him I demand to see the Welfare and he takes me to the office.

'You're not due a visit from your social worker,' he says.

'But I want to see her.'

'You can wait until she comes.'

'I want to see her now!'

'You can't see her now.'

'How no?'

'Because you can't!'

'You can phone her,' I say.

'What do you want to speak to her about?'

'About my Dad.'

He's puzzled. 'Your Dad?

'Aye.'

'What about your Dad?'

'I want to see him.'

'What do you mean you want to see him? Who's been talking to you about your Dad?'

'My Uncle and Auntie.'

'Your Uncle and Auntie?'

'Aye.'

'What Uncle and Auntie?'

'I saw them.'

'You saw them?'

'Aye.'

'When did you see them?'

'Today.'

'Today?'

'Aye, this afternoon, in Lundin Links.'

'In Lundin Links?'

'Aye, and they told me he lives in Dundee and they gave me an address for him.'

'Did they now?'

'Aye, and my Dad's no keeping well and I want to see him. So phone the Welfare!'

I tell Specky Boy that I've seen my Auntie and Uncle and I tell him about my Dad living in Dundee and that I'm going to ask the Welfare if I can get to visit him. He says that he would like to see the Welfare too because he's sick of Uncle Dave and he wants shifted out the place.

'Do you no like it here Specky Boy?'

'I hate the place,' he says.

I keep on at Uncle Dave for weeks about my father. He says he's telephoned the Welfare and that there's no more he can do for now. He says that I'll just have to wait until my social worker gets the time to visit me.

I fall out with the Maths teacher at school and he's planning to belt me. He's a wee baldy man that keeps his strap on his shoulder, under his jacket, and nobody likes him because he's handy with that strap and half the time he belts bairns for bugger all.

'Come out here,' he shouts to me. I pay him no heed and just sit tight and he comes to my desk. 'Put your hand on the desk,' he says, then he whacks it with the belt. I just look at him and he whacks me again and again. I look at my palms and they're stinging and red. The weals have started to rise on my wrists as he walks away. 'You're as bad as your brothers!' he shouts.

'My brothers?'

He turns. 'Oh, you can talk. I thought you were a dummy!'

'What brothers? What were their names?'

'Is this boy a fool or what?' The eyes of the class are on me now. 'Did you ever meet a boy that doesn't know the names of his own brothers?' He's back at my desk and leaning over me when he says, 'Your tinky mother dropped so many fucking bairns that even she wouldn't know half their names!'

I'm on my feet quick and kick the desk over and my wooden chair's in bits when it smacks off the wall and I've never seen a man shift so quick in my life. The classroom door is near off the hinges when I slam it behind me, a lad gets a punch in the pus in the corridor and four windows are smashed with stones on my way out the playground.

I walk to Pittenweem and I'm looking at the boats in the harbour when Uncle Dave and a man I've not seen before get a grip of me. I'm got by the neck and piled into Uncle Dave's van and he drives while the other man pins me to the floor in the back.

At the home the other man buggers off and Uncle Dave takes me straight to his bedroom where I get a real good hiding. He whacks me again and again on the bare arse with a leather strap. At first I howl like a banshee, then I shut up and just grit my teeth and wait for him to finish. I get a few more whacks then he stops. I stand up and he's looking at me and I'm looking at him.

'I lost my temper a bit,' he says.

'Aye.'

'I didn't mean to hurt you Sandy.' He comes over and kneels down in front of me. He puts his arms round me and feels my arse cheeks with his hands. I start to pull my shorts up and he stops me doing this. So, I just stand and let him look at me.

'Can I go now?'

'You can go when I say.'

'But I want to go now!'

'I said you can go when I say!'

'Fuck off!' I'm raging.

Big mistake. He's raging too. He grabs me and forces me face down on the bed. He presses my face into the pillow and I can hardly get a fucking breath. He whips down his shorts and gets a good grip of my wrists. He's on my back and forcing my legs apart with his knees. He's hard and pressing at my arse and I'm in no doubt about what he's trying to do. I'm absolutely petrified. For a split second everything goes black and my head starts to spin. Suddenly the black turns to red – a red mist! I'm fucking raging, and a voice screams in my head – kill kill kill! A power surges through my entire body and I push upwards, lifting him on my back. Suddenly, I slam back to the mattress with a thud, and my teeth sink into his right wrist. He lets out a shriek and slaps me round the ear with his free hand. But I continue to bite down as hard as I possibly can, and I taste the sweetness of his blood as it oozes into my mouth. He slaps me a few more times, but I still clamp down on his wrist. He grips my hair and pulls my head back, at the same time wrenching his wrist from my mouth and he's free.

'Fuck!' he shouts, and that was the first, and only time, that I ever heard Uncle Dave swear.

He goes to his bathroom and I can hear the tap running as I pull up my shorts. He comes back in the room with a handkerchief wrapped tightly round his wrist. He watches me in stunned silence as I leave the room.

One day a woman speaks to me at her gate. 'Is your name Reid?' she says.

'Aye, how?'

'Because you look like a lad that used to be in that home before you arrived and his name was Reid too.'

'Maybe it was my brother.'

'Do you have a brother called Donald?' she asks.

'Aye, that'll be him.'

'You don't sound very sure.'

'I've never seen him before.'

'You've never seen him?'

'No.'

She offers me a fag and when I refuse she says Donald liked to smoke. She lights it and hands it to me. I start puffing and blow the smoke in the air and she tells me more about Donald. She says he mentioned that he had brothers and sisters but she can't remember their names. I tell her that the Welfare tells me bugger all about my family and she says that's a shame. She says to come to her door anytime I like.

When Miss Black finally visits I ask her to take me out the place and she drives me round to the harbour. 'Is there something you want to talk to me about Sandy?'

'Aye.'

'What?'

'My Dad.'

'Your Dad!'

'Aye, I want to visit him.'

She looks surprised. I ask if Uncle Dave has told her that I want to see my Dad and she says that he hasn't.

'He phoned you about it?'

'No, he hasn't phoned me about it Sandy.'

'Are you sure?'

'Of course I'm sure.'

'He told me he'd phoned you about it.'

'Well I can assure you he hasn't. Maybe it slipped his mind.'

'Aye.'

'He is a busy man after all.'

'Aye.'

'We're all busy people,' she says looking at her watch.

'So can I go and see him?'

'Who's been telling you about your Dad, Sandy?'

'My Uncle Sandy and Auntie Peggy.'

'Is that the Aunt and Uncle you met when you were at Ovenstone?'

'Aye.'

'Have you seen them again?'

'Aye, they bide in a wood next to Lundin Links now and I've been to visit them.'

'Did Uncle Dave take you there?'

'No, I went myself, on my bike.'

'I see.'

'I have an address for him. Can I visit him?'

'I'm not sure.'

'What do you mean you're not sure?'

'I'll have to look into it.'

'Well look into it then.'

'I'll need to check that that's a proper address you have for him first.'

'It is a proper address. I got it from my Auntie and Uncle.'

'Why do you want to see your father all of a sudden?'

'It's not all of a sudden.'

'It seems that way to me.'

'I've often asked you about my father and you've always said that you don't know anything about him. You said you didn't know where he was and that he could be anywhere. Well, I've got an address for him now and I want to see him!'

'I'll look into it and get back to you once I've done that.'

'How long will that be?'

'I don't know. Things like this can take time Sandy.'

'Well don't take long. Because if you don't take me, I'll run away from this place and visit him myself!'

'I said I'll look into it.'

'How's my sister?'

'She's fine.'

'Have you seen her?'

'Yes, she's at the nursing college now and doing fine.'

'When did you see her?'

'About a fortnight ago.'

'Why did you not take me?'

'Well, it wasn't exactly an arranged visit Sandy. I was in Aberdeen on some other business and I managed to look in on Maggie after that. She said to tell you that she was asking for you.'

'Aye, well, when you see her again tell her I was asking for her too.'

'Is there anything else?' She's keen to get going now.

'Aye.'

'What?'

'I don't like Uncle Dave.'

'Oh, why not?'

'Because he hits me with a belt.'

'Uncle Dave's a wonderful man and if he belted you then you must have done something to deserve it.'

'He belts all the laddies in St Margaret's.'

'Well, it must be hard looking after so many boys. And he'll need to take a firm line with boys when they misbehave. I think the reason you don't like him is because he doesn't let you do as you please and keeps you in line. Anyway, it's time I was getting you back to St Margaret's now.'

'One more thing.'

'What?'

'Why do I have to wear short trousers all the time? We're the only bairns in the whole school that have to wear them and the other bairns just laugh at us.'

'You look very smart in short trousers, Sandy.'

'I'm fourteen!'

'What difference does that make?'

'I don't care about looking smart. I just want to be the same as all the other bairns at school and wear long trousers.'

'That's something you'll have to discuss with Uncle Dave.'

'You discuss it with him.'

'I can't tell Uncle Dave what you've to wear.'

'Then why should he tell me what I've to wear?'

'Because that's the way it is. Uncle Dave's in charge at St Margaret's, not you Sandy Reid!'

'Aye.'

'Now is there anything else?'

'No, just take me back to St Margaret's.'

I've known I was going to see my father for about a week now and for the last few days I've hardly slept a wink. They have me dressed in my Sunday best for this visit and I've got short trousers, ankle socks, a shirt and a grey jumper on. Miss Black drives me to Dundee and when we get to the place my jaw drops. I've never seen anything like this in my life before. The place is a mess with rubbish strewn all over the street. You would think an aeroplane had flown over and dropped a couple of bombs on the place. Some of the buildings are falling to bits and there's plenty smashed windows. Miss Black stops the car and points to a house across the street.

'That's where your father lives,' she says. 'Go over and chap the door, they're expecting you.'

'Are you coming with me?'

'This will be the first time you've seen your father Sandy. I think it would be better for you to see him on your own without me being there. I'll come back for you in an hour.'

I cross the street and she drives off. I knock the door and a wee stocky man answers. 'Are you Sandy?' he says.

'Aye.'

'God bless us. The last time I saw you, you were a wee bairn!'

'Aye.'

'Do you know who I am?'

222

'No.'

'I'm your own brother – your brother Henry!'

He puts his arm round my shoulders and takes me into the living room. There's a few wild looking boys in this room and they all look at me. He tells me that most of them are my cousins. They don't say much, but look pleased enough to see me.

An old man sits sleeping in a chair next to a gas fire. 'Is that my father?' I say.

'No, he's upstairs. He doesn't keep well and lies in his bed most of the time. Come with me and I'll let you see him.'

We go upstairs. 'It's me, Father. I've got Sandy to see you,' he says.

The curtains are drawn, the room's dark and I can hardly make anything out.

'Is that you son?'

'Aye it's me.'

'Light the candle Henry.'

Henry strikes a match and I see my father's face for the first time.

'I'm Sandy.'

'I know who you are. See a smoke from you Henry.'

Henry rolls a fag and hands it to him. 'Put on a drop tea for me.'

'There's no gas Dad.'

'Put a shilling in the meter then!'

'Nobody has a shilling.'

'No electric and no fucking gas!'

'I've got a shilling.'

I fumble in my pocket and hand the shilling to him.

'Give it to your brother,' he says.

Henry goes to make tea and I'm left with him now. He lights the fag and draws heavily. When Henry comes back with tea he's sleeping and we leave the room.

Henry takes me back to the kitchen and says. 'Your father's not well Sandy.'

'No.'

'He's worn out son.'

'Aye.'

'That's how he never had much to say.'

'Aye.'

'He just sleeps most of the time.'

'Aye.'

'Did you like him?'

'Aye, I liked him.'

'Is it St Margaret's home you're in?'

'Aye.'

'I was in that place too.'

'Were you?'

'Aye, I went through all their homes. Is it still David Murphy that runs that place?'

'Aye, Uncle Dave.'

'Aye, we called him Uncle Dave too. That bastard got me put to an approved school.'

'Did he?'

'Aye. Watch yourself with that man Sandy. He's a poofter!'

'Aye.'

'He's handy with the belt too.'

'Aye, he belts all the laddies in there.'

'He likes to mess about with young laddies. Don't you let him near you Sandy.'

A man comes in the kitchen and says the Welfare's waiting outside for me.

I'm in the car and Miss Black asks how the meeting went with my father and I say it went fine. She asks if I want to go back and visit him some other time and I say that I do.

* * *

I've got a rabbit in my arms and its bairns are sliding out the back of it and landing on the stone floor. Aunt Margaret comes along. 'That thing's giving birth!' she roars.

'Aye.'

She runs to get help and I'm left standing with this thing that I don't know what to do with. So I toss it outside.

I go looking for Uncle Dave and see Specky Boy coming out his bedroom. He's upset and runs downstairs.

'That rabbit's had babies,' I say.

'Has it?'

'Aye, I think Aunt Margaret's looking at it. What's wrong with Specky Boy?'

'Never mind him,' Uncle Dave says.

I tell him about the bairns dropping out the rabbit and falling onto the stone floor and he says not to worry about that because Aunt Margaret will know what to do with it. I ask again about Specky Boy and he says that he was misbehaving. I go looking for Specky Boy and find him next to the boat shed.

'Did you get the belt?' I ask him.

'Aye.'

'What for?'

'For nothing.'

'That man gives you no peace. Let's see the marks.'

'What marks?'

'The marks of the belt you fool.'

'I . . . I never really got the belt.'

'What do you mean you never really got the belt?'

'Well, not much.'

'What were you crying for then? What did he do to you?'

'Nothing,' he says, and buggers off.

I tell Uncle Dave that I want to see my sister Maggie. I ask him to phone the Welfare to arrange a visit for me and he says that I can't just go around demanding things all the time.

People are not going to jump every time you want something he says. I tell him that I want to tell Maggie about my visit to my father and he says I'll just have to wait until I'm due a visit from the Welfare.

'I want to see my sister soon.'

'You'll just have to wait.'

'Phone the Welfare.'

'I'm not phoning them. They'll be thinking I'm never off the phone to them!'

'You never phoned them about my Dad!'

'Yes I did.'

'No you didn't! Miss Black told me that you never phoned her. She said that's why she never came to see me for so long.'

'That's not true!'

'Aye it is.'

'Are you calling me a liar?'

'Aye – you're a fucking liar!'

'Don't you swear at me lad – come here!'

I'm off like a shot.

I'm on the beach and he's not bothered to come after me. I'm fourteen now and the sooner I get out this place the better. I'm fed up with the school. I'm fed up wearing short trousers and looking a fool all the time. I'm fed up with Uncle Dave, this place and all the people in it, bar Specky Boy. I'm fed up having to ask the Welfare before I can do anything and I'm fed up begging to visit my own sister. I want to leave the school and get a job and stay somewhere else. I want to visit my sister, my father and my brother Henry whenever I like. If I run away from this place I could stay with Sandy and Peggy in their wee tent, and if the police come looking for me I can hide in the wood and they would never find me.

The Welfare arranges for me to see Maggie and the visit's to be done in a day. It takes the whole morning to get to

Aberdeen and when I get there my sister's pleased to see me. Miss Black leaves me with Maggie and her new boyfriend. I don't pay much attention to him and he doesn't have much to say to me. He just sits quiet and lets me and her get on with things. She's grown up now and looks different. She tells me that she's training to be a nurse and I tell her that I went to see our father. I start to tell her about him, but she's not interested.

'Do you not want to hear about your own father Maggie?'

'I don't care about him Sandy.'

'How no?'

'Because I don't.'

'But he's your father.'

'I don't care.'

'But you used to go on about our family all the time.'

'Aye, that's was when I was little.'

'I saw one of our brothers too.'

'Did you?'

'Aye.'

'Which one?'

'Henry. Are you interested in him?'

'No.'

'How no?'

'Because I'm not!'

'So you've lost interest in our whole family now?'

'Aye.'

'How?'

'Because they lost interest in us a long time ago!'

'But Maggie . . .'

'What?'

'Our Mammy came to the school to see you and you said that was a good thing.'

'Aye, and that was the last I saw of her. She never bothered to come back again. I don't give a fuck about her. I don't give a fuck about our father, or our uncles and aunties. I don't give a fuck about any of them!'

'Do you give a fuck about me Maggie?'

'Aye, of course I do.'

'It won't matter about our Mammy now anyway.'

'How no?'

'Because she's dead.'

'What do you mean she's dead?'

'She died.'

'Who told you that?'

'Our Uncle and Auntie.'

'What Uncle and Auntie?'

'Uncle Sandy and Auntie Peggy. They were camped in the wood at Ovenstone and they told me our Mammy was dead. That was a while back.'

'Was it?'

'Aye, I told Miss Black. Did she no tell you?'

'That woman tells me bugger all. I never even knew you were in St Margaret's until a few weeks ago.'

'She never tells me much either Maggie.'

'I hate Miss Black. All that woman cares about is herself. She gets good money to look after bairns like us and she does bugger all to earn it.'

'What do you mean Maggie?'

'She makes a good living out the suffering of bairns and I've got no time for her.'

'I don't think much of her either Maggie. She never brings me to see you and she never listens to a word I say.'

'I'm no bothered because I'll be done with her soon.'

'What do you mean?'

'I'm getting married.'

'Married!'

'Aye, to him.'

'Your boyfriend?'

'Aye.'

'When?'

'Soon. And once I'm married the Welfare will have nothing more to do with me and I can do what I like.'

'What about me Maggie?'

'Don't worry Sandy. I'll get a house and you can come and live with me.'

'I'll see about getting you a job,' her boyfriend says.

'A job?'

'Aye, he's a fisherman,' Maggie says. 'And he's going to see about getting you started at the trawling school here in Aberdeen. That's where you train to be a fisherman.'

'Is it?'

'Aye, and when you leave the school you can work on the fishing boats and bide with us when you're ashore.'

'Can I no leave the school early and start right away on a fishing boat Maggie?'

'No you have to put your time in at the school first. But you don't have long to go now Sandy. And when you leave the school you'll be coming straight up here to start a new life and we'll be together again.'

'Aye.'

'And there's more yet,' she says.

'What?'

'You're going to be an uncle too.'

'An uncle?'

'Aye, I'm going to have a baby.'

'A baby!'

'Aye, and he's the father.'

I look at him and that lad looks as proud as punch.

I tell Miss Black all that Maggie's told me, bar the bits about her getting married and having a bairn, because she's told me not to. Miss Black says not to build my hopes up because I might not be allowed to move to Aberdeen. I tell her that I want to be a fisherman, like Maggie's boyfriend and she says that she'll have to look into that.

Uncle Dave comes to me one day and says that since I'm nearly fifteen he's going to give me my own room now. I get my stuff and he takes me up the stairs to the very top of the building. We go into a room that I've never been in before. It's only a wee room, with a single bed and a chest of drawers. You could get nothing else in this room if you tried, because it's that small. You get a rare view from the window and I like the idea of having a room to myself and not having to share with anyone. I can do what I like up here. If I get fed up with the other lads I can just come up here and lie on my bed and look out the window. And there's no one to bother you. No one except Uncle Dave.

I'm lying on my bed one night when he comes into the room. He sits on the bed and asks if I like having a room all to myself and I say that I do.

'Do you know why I've given you this room Sandy?'

'Aye, because I'm older now.'

'That's right. You're a senior boy.'

'Aye.'

'And not just that. You're my favourite boy as well.'

'What do you mean?'

'You're my favourite boy in this place now. You must know that?'

'Aye.'

'And you can do what you like up here. You have your own television set and you can watch a film in your bed if you like.'

'Aye.'

He puts his arm round my shoulders and tells me that he's always liked me better than any of the other boys in this place. He says that's why he was so lenient with me when I misbehaved, and hardly gave me the belt when other boys got leathered for much less. I say that he batters some of the bairns for bugger all and he says that's not true. Anytime he used the belt on them they deserved it, he says. He pushes me down on the bed and tries to kiss me and I don't like that and push him back.

'Don't worry about anything. You'll be fine Sandy,' he says. He gets more forceful and puts his full weight on me. I'm raging but he pays no heed and tries to kiss me again.

'Fuck off!' I roar, and start to kick my legs.

'You'll be fine Sandy. Just keep quiet.' He starts to pull my shorts down.

'Fuck off you bastard!' I'm going mental and kicking like a mule, but he's too strong for me. He puts his hand over my mouth to stop me roaring and I can hardly get a breath because he's covering my nose too.

This time he's ready for me and he has me in a vice-like grip which I find it impossible to escape from. I try desperately to summon the strength that I managed to find the last time he attacked me. But I can't – I'm just too weak. I feel weightless on the mattress. Unsolid, almost as if I'm floating. His hand presses firmly against my inner thigh and my legs part effort-lessly. He lowers his head and plants kisses on my neck as he presses against me. It's as if I'm anaesthetized and I feel no pain, only shame, as he grunts and enters me. The tears roll silently down my cheeks as I close my eyes and listen to the gentle voice in my head.

My eyes open and he's pulling up his shorts.

'My brother was right about you,' I hiss.

'Be quiet Sandy!'

'You're a fucking poof!' I'm off the bed and on my feet.

'Ssssh Sandy – be quiet . . .'

'You're a fucking poof!' My voice is raised.

'Be quiet!'

I drop to my knees and take the legs from him and his head

batters off the door. I'm in with kicks and punches. He reacts quick and gets me in a bear hug. He lifts me clean off my feet and pins me to the wall. I can't move and my fists are useless. So I nut the bastard and burst his nose.

'Calm down – calm down Sandy!'

'My brother said you were a fucking poof!'

'And what happened to him?

'What?'

'I got him put to an approved school. That's what!'

'Aye, he told me.'

'And I can do the same with you.'

'What?'

'Do you want to go to an approved school?'

I don't answer him and he loosens his grip on me. He tells me that all it takes is word from him and I'll be packed straight off to an approved school. He says it will be like a living hell in one of those places, that I will be locked up in a cell all day long and probably never get out the place until I'm eighteen. I turn to look out the window and he leaves the room. He's an evil bastard but I'm powerless to do anything here. I just need to try and keep away from him and get out of here as fast as I can.

I apply for the trawling school in Aberdeen. You have to be fifteen to get into that school so I won't be able to get in until I leave the school. Miss Black says that if I'm accepted then I'll have to stay at the seaman's mission in Aberdeen because I won't be allowed to stay with Maggie. And she says that she'll arrange with the Welfare in Aberdeen to keep an eye on me when I'm there.

I've been thinking about my Dad and ask the Welfare if I can see him again. And I want to talk to my brother Henry about Uncle Dave. When we arrive at my Dad's house she drops me off and says she'll be back in an hour. I knock the door and get no answer. I look through the living-room window but can't see anyone. I wonder if my Dad's maybe lying in his bed upstairs and can't get to the door.

The woman next door opens her window. 'Who are you looking for?' she says.

'My Dad.'

'Who's your Dad?'

'Henry Reid.'

'Old Henry?'

'Aye.'

'He died son.'

'Did he?'

'Aye, and the rest of them moved out.'

She shuts the window and I sit down on the stone step to wait for Miss Black. I hardly knew the man but that's him and my Mammy both dead now and I'm not even fifteen. Doesn't seem fair that I won't get to know either of them now when things could have been so different. I know I just have to get on with my own life now and get away from Uncle Dave.

I get word that I've been accepted for the trawling school. Miss Black says that she's got me a place at the seaman's mission and that I won't be staying with Maggie. I ask why I can't stay with my sister and she says that Maggie has enough to be getting on with now that she has a husband and a baby to look after.

Five days before my fifteenth birthday I leave the school. No more short trousers for me. Three days later Uncle Dave takes me into the office and tells me that I'll be leaving St Margaret's in the morning. I go to find Specky Boy.

'I'm leaving this place for good tomorrow.'

'Are you?'

'Aye.'

'I wish I was leaving too Sandy.'

'I'm starting at the trawling school in Aberdeen. When I'm finished with that I'll be on a fishing boat and you get plenty money for that. That's me finished with Uncle Dave and this place.'

'The Welfare keep you until you're eighteen,' he says.

'Aye, but they don't bother you if you're working, so I'll be fine.'

'When I leave school I'll do the same as you Sandy.'

'Aye, you can apply for the trawling school like I did.'

'Where would I stay?'

'You'll get a bed in the seaman's mission like me.'

He looks at me and I look at him.

'I'm going to miss you Specky Boy.'

'I'll miss you too Sandy Boy.'

The next morning I'm up early and standing in the office. Uncle Dave hands me a letter of introduction to give to the captain at the seaman's mission. I get money to keep me going for a few days in Aberdeen along with my saving stamps that he says I can cash at any post office in Aberdeen. He lifts his keys and a shoebox from the desktop and we go to the van. He turns right and goes up the street. We pass the post office, the Golf Hotel and the bank. He turns in the main street and parks across from the church. He cuts the engine and we sit in silence.

'That's your bus coming now.'

'Aye,' I open the door.

He hands me the shoebox. 'You've nothing to come back for now.'

I look at him and he looks at me. Then I'm off and straight onto the bus.

'A single to Aberdeen, mister.'

'I only go as far as Dundee son.'

'A single to Dundee then!'

The driver tells me that I'll have an hour to wait in Dundee for the Aberdeen bus. And that the whole journey will take over five hours. I get my ticket and sit at the back of the bus. We leave Elie and start along the coast. I watch the fields, the trees and the hedgerows whizzing past. No more 'Home boy'. No more short trousers. No more David Murphy! I'm relaxed, happy and free.

My eyes fall on the sea. I'd never given a thought to next week, tomorrow, or even the next fucking hour. Now my mind starts to race. I'm thinking about what lies ahead and all manner of thoughts flood my brain. My mouth's dry and I don't have a drink. I wish Maggie was on this bus. Right now I would even take the Greenbanks matron sitting next to me. Other bairns go back to their own people when they leave children's homes. Their mammy's are waiting with open arms at the bus station for them. There will be no mammy waiting at the bus station for me. Because there is no mammy – she's fucking dead.

What does it matter anyway? Maggie said she never bothered her arse to come back for us and that she never cared. But Peggy and Sandy told me she was never done looking for her bairns and was always fighting to get us back. I remember the night in the tent and Peggy's words come back to me. 'If you said to her, "What are you looking at Mary?" she would say, "A wee picture that my laddie drew at the school." And she kept that picture with her until the day she died. She would never part with that picture.'

My heart pounds in my chest and I can hardly get a breath. My head's so full of questions that I think it's going to explode. Why was I in the homes? Why did she not come back for me? Why didn't she care? What does it matter? I'll never know, because the woman can't tell me when she's dead. But I'm alive, and somehow I've survived the foster families, separation from my sister and Uncle Dave. I don't know what the future holds but it's a new life with new hope and now, for the first time ever, I'm in charge of what happens to me. And that feels good.

My palms are sweating and I grip the shoebox on my lap. I look down and wonder what's in it so I open it. It's packed full with letters that the Welfare has already opened and I think I know who they are from, but I'm scared to open them in case the disappointment kills me. There's also a bundle of ten shilling notes as thick as your wrist, out of date and no use to me now, but I don't care. Every envelope has Master Sandy Reid on the front and every letter is signed Mum.

It was hard to make it through those years without
    you by my side,
It was hard to take what they threw at me with no
    place for to hide,
But always in my darkest hour I'd hear you in my
    ear,
And once you'd dried my silent tears you'd whisper
    – Mummy's here.